Silver Link Silk Editions
SLP

A World of Rail

Railways of Europe and beyond

At Gare du Nord station, Paris, 'Pacific' No 231-H-684 receives its daily maintenance before starting work. These engines, built from 1914 onwards, received rebuilds and ran into the 1960s, hauling some of the famous 'Fleche d'Or' expresses from Calais to Paris.

Silver Link Silk Editions

SLP

A World of Rail
Railways of Europe and beyond

John Legg and Ian Peaty

Silver Link Publishing Ltd

First published in 2017

British Library Cataloguing in Publication Data

A catalogue record for this book is available from the British Library.

ISBN 978 1 85794 485 3

Silver Link Publishing Ltd
The Trundle
Ringstead Road
Great Addington
Kettering
Northants NN14 4BW

Tel/Fax: 01536 330588
email: sales@nostalgiacollection.com
Website: www.nostalgiacollection.com

Printed and bound in the Czech Republic

Back cover: On the island of Sardinia, a mixed train crosses a viaduct on the Arbatax branch line to the east coast, hauled by a 2-6-2T locomotive built by Reggio Emilia in 1931. *Ian Peaty*

Introduction

Whether we are younger or older, aware of the fact or not, railways have played an important part in all of our lives since the 1830s, which was the start of railways as we know them today, although it is difficult to see how a steam hauled train of those times relates to today's streamlined, highly technical, electric/diesel hauled passenger and freight trains.

From those early days Britain's expertise was soon to influence and build railways in countries around the world that had never seen or heard of a railway before. Some of these railway networks are still in existence today, proving that Victorian engineering was of the highest quality.

In some areas, especially in Europe, inter-city travel can mean a seamless journey, sitting in the same train, through several neighbouring countries to a final destination. This involves specially built locomotives that can cope with changing power and signalling arrangements.

Then there are the preserved railways, saved from neglect and decay by enthusiastic volunteers. Railways such as these now thrive around the world with a wide range of steam and classic diesel locomotives.

Lastly, there are the railway lines that have been closed many years and almost buried by the onset of nature. There is often plenty to see with infrastructures still in place, albeit neglected, such as stations, track, signals, derelict rolling stock etc.

Railways have touched our lives in many ways, and more recently through railway holidays abroad that can suit the enthusiast or the holiday maker who just enjoys riding the train and taking in spectacular scenery.

Over the years the authors have travelled to many places abroad and have accumulated an extensive amount of unique photographs of railways both old and new. A selection of these are in this book and include what may be termed the more unusual, individual, or perhaps the more quirky aspects of railways.

We hope you enjoy turning the pages of our book revealing not only the modern, but the nostalgia of times gone by, the history of lost lines and many varied and unique aspects of the World's railways, all given birth from the industrial revolution in Great Britain and the engineering developments over the last 180 years, much of it seen on our travels over the past 40 years.

Contents

France

France was a late developer when it came to building its railways. It is a large country and by the start of the 19th century was still mainly agricultural, showing little signs of industrialisation. The French Government wanted to be involved in the building of railways, but had no clear policy in view, which suppressed the free-market approach that was then raging in Britain. By the 1840s little progress had been made, with just a few small railways having been constructed. Eventually, in 1842 legislation was passed that virtually put the French Government in control of developing the French network, although the railways were still privately owned. It was a 'halfway house' between the free market and nationalisation.

The first main-line railway opened in 1843 between Gare St Lazare in Paris and Rouen in Normandy. British expertise and experience was called upon and the 28 miles of track and its infrastructure were

A French poster advertising the connecting boat trains of the London, Chatham & Dover Railway, the South Eastern Railway and the French Chemins de Fer du Nord from London to Paris. *Ian Peaty*

A real 'old timer', an 0-6-0 tender engine built between 1867 and 1886, series 533 and 860, at Quimper, Brittany in 1948. One of this class is preserved at the large museum at Mulhouse.

engineered by Joseph Locke, with construction contracted to Thomas Brassey, who was responsible for building many railways in Great Britain and across the world.

By 1914 the French railway network had become so dense that it gave access to almost every town and village, utilising a vast narrow-gauge network operating from junctions on main lines. There were around 37,500 miles (60,000km) of track, of which about one-third was narrow gauge.

During the 1930s the narrow-gauge lines were closing, leaving the network reduced to around 25,000 miles (40,000km). By this time operating companies were struggling financially and the system was nationalised in 1938 by the Socialist Government to become Société Nationale de Chemin de fer Francais (SNCF).

Following the devastation wreaked upon its railways during the Second World War, France has rebuilt and electrified most of its main lines

Brittany had a considerable metre-gauge network, and the Reseau Breton railway at Carhaix was its hub. Mallet 0-6-0+0-6-0T No E.416 rests beside a typical water tank.

A metre-gauge Corpet Louvet 0-6-0T crosses a typical Brittany viaduct with a mixed train in the early 1950s. *Ian Peaty*

and from the 1970s has been constructing and upgrading its high-speed network across the country, mainly radiating from Paris and providing a fast and direct service to its major areas and cities.

However, the area of France is nearly three times that of the United Kingdom and still requires an extremely large network (17,414 miles/28,025km) of conventional primary and secondary lines to provide rail services across the country.

Left: A closer view of the 'Pacific' at Rouen highlights the plethora of external pipework and domes so common on continental steam locomotives – an impressive piece of machinery.

Below: Two diesels, Nos 469209 and 469228, idle at Carpentras in Provence, the terminus of a 15km freight line from Sorgues, north of Avignon. The Fret Class BB 46000 series was built in 2006 in Valencia, Spain.

Rouen station is built between a series of tunnels in this medieval city. On the left is a Renault Type ABJ3 railcar of 1935/9 with the massive air unit hump over the cab, while on the right is a 4-6-2 'Pacific'.

Chemin de Fer Touristique du Tarn

A narrow-gauge 1ft 7¾in (500mm) tramway has been laid over the former 600mm-gauge railway formation of the Tramway à Vapeur du Tarn (TVT), which was built in 1895 and closed on 11 May 1937. The former steam railway ran south from St Sulpice, which is a standard-gauge junction on the line running north-east from Toulouse to Albi. The main-line junction branches off in an eastward direction along the Agout valley to Castres in the foothills of the Languedoc Hills. The smaller feeder narrow-gauge followed much the same direction and served the farming community.

In 1975 a group of preservationists, some of whom were also aero engineers at Toulouse, formed ACOVA to reinstate a railway on part of the track formation. The previous TVT station at St Lieux-les-Lavaur was intact, so this was the starting point for the new line. On leaving the terminus the line crosses over a village road and runs between houses in a manner that was once commonplace. On the outskirts of the village a workshop area has been built, which includes both 500mm and 600mm track and engine sheds. Here the volunteers have built a Schioma 0-4-0 diesel utilising a former colliery locomotive found in Catalonia, Spain. Several of the coaches used on tourist trains were also built here.

Continuing along the single track, after only a short distance the train crosses the River Agout by a fine viaduct 132 metres long, which is shared

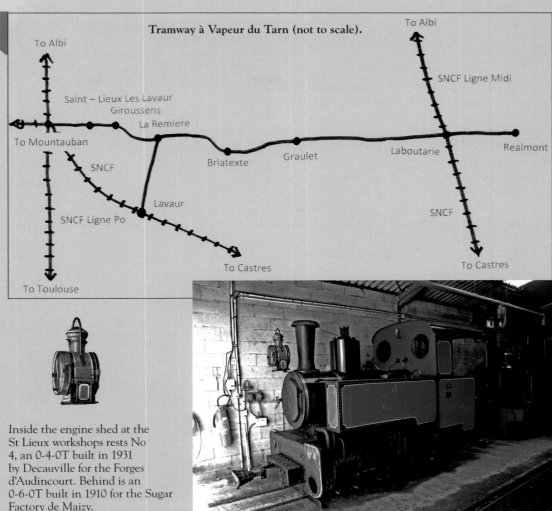

Tramway à Vapeur du Tarn (not to scale).

To Albi
To Albi
SNCF Ligne Midi
Saint – Lieux Les Lavaur
Giroussens
La Remiere
To Mountauban
SNCF
Briatexte
Graulet
Laboutarie
Realmont
Lavaur
SNCF
SNCF Ligne Po
To Castres
To Toulouse
To Castres

Inside the engine shed at the St Lieux workshops rests No 4, an 0-4-0T built in 1931 by Decauville for the Forges d'Audincourt. Behind is an 0-6-0T built in 1910 for the Sugar Factory de Maizy.

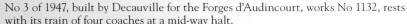

No 3 of 1947, built by Decauville for the Forges d'Audincourt, works No 1132, rests with its train of four coaches at a mid-way halt.

The terminus station at St Lieux was built on the former standard-gauge branch line, viewed here from the road level crossing protected by a British-built signal and warning bell. The Crochat 14L diesel is at the platform.

with road vehicles. The line then gradually climbs through pleasant countryside until it arrives at Martels. This is a beautiful landscaped garden and nursery and makes for a pleasant stop before returning to St Lieux. Trains operate between April and October.

Steam locos consist of Couillet 0-6-0 No 1576,

built in 1910 and liveried in black with red frames. This loco previously worked at the Sugar Factory de Maizy. Given the number 4 is an 0-4-0 tank built in 1931 by Decauville, works No 1111, which weighs 5 tonnes and is ex-Forges d'Audincourt. This is painted black with bright blue panels lined out in cream. Another Decauville four-

wheeler is works No 1132 built in 1947. A British-built Ruston 50hp diesel, originally supplied to Usines Von Roll, a steelworks in Gerlafingen, Switzerland, in 1965, is painted bright green with a bonnet headlight – and still looks British! Crochat 14L diesel No 8, built in 1919, is liveried in red. Coaching stock includes the four built by the local group, all four-wheelers, and two enclosed bogie coaches built by Giragr, replicas from the former TVT line. These were built by Decauville to the KE type built in the 1920s. Two Baguley-built coaches supplied to Butlin's Holiday Camp at Clacton, Essex, in 1947, were adapted by Alan Keef to suit the French gauge; they are both 32-seaters.

In the engineering workshops on the outskirts of St Lieux are an impish little diesel beside the Decauville 0-6-0 tank built in 1931.

A train is about to depart from St Lieux with the Decauville 0-4-0T No 3 waiting for the last passenger to board.

Train à Vapeur des Cevennes (CITEV)

The Cevennes region of wooded hills and limestone gorges is situated on the south-west bank of the River Rhone. Due west of Avignon, famous for its Roman aqueduct, is the former coal-mining area centred on Ales. In 1881 La Compagnie des Chemin de Fer Paris-Lyons-Méditerranée (PLM) opened one of the few standard-gauge secondary railways from Ales, then a developing coal-mining area, to Anduze in the Gardon River valley. In 1903 the line was extended to St Jean-du-Gard, due west of Ales, and further into the mountainous region. The terrain was challenging to the engineers but the incentive of opening up further coal extraction areas sped them onwards. The line, now operated by the CITEV from Anduze to St Jean-du-Gard, consists of four tunnels, several stone-built viaducts and a major steel bridge of 104 metres spanning the river on the approaches to Anduze – all major constructions within an overall length of 13 kilometres!

Above right: German-built 0-8-0 tank No 1751, from the Krupp stable, was built in 1937 to haul local coal trains from the mountainous inland to St Jean-du-Gard.

Right: Standard-gauge 0-6-0 diesel No 325 was built by Gaston Moyse of Paris, Type 20 TDE, in 1951. Window 'eyelashes' were obligatory!

Far right: At St Jean-du-Gard station is a Renault diesel railcar, for 2nd Class only, built as Type VH-24 in 1933. A total of 91 were built for service in the South of France.

The extension was opened for freight and passenger traffic in May 1909, the delay caused by heavy building works on embankments to alleviate torrents of water and flooding. The scant passenger service was withdrawn in the mid-1940s, with freight, chiefly coal, finally ceasing in July 1971. For some 12 years the line lay abandoned until the railway preservationists in the guise of the Train à Vapeur des Cevennes became established. In 1986 a new organisation, the Compagnie Internationale des Trains Express a Vapeur (CITEV,) took over and has gone on from strength to strength in its professional operation of running this railway.

The train journey takes 40 minutes, running through spectacular scenery of deep wooded valleys crossing the curved viaducts and storming through the tunnels, from St Jean-du-Gard station, at an elevation of 189m, down to Anduze, at 134m. Between the Tunnel de Prafrance (114 metres) and the two viaducts and the Anduze Tunnel (833 metres) is the Bambouseraie, the largest bamboo garden and nursery in Europe, good views of which are provided by the elevated railway. The railway employs 14 people, with volunteers assisting in the operating season of 1 April to 1 November. Four trains a day run in each direction.

The railway has both steam and diesel locomotives at its disposal and a Renault classic SNCF auto railcar.

Previous page: Typical limestone scenery, with a six-coach train hauled by the Krupp 0-8-0T crossing the viaduct over the Gardon d'Anduze River between St Jean-du-Gard and Anduze.

0-8-0T No 1751 runs round its train at Anduze. The picture also shows the portal of the long tunnel, which exits at the north of the town directly onto a girder bridge.

Chemin de Fer du Vivrais

The Chemin de Fer du Vivrais was a part of the Interet General, an outcome of the Plan Freyuey of 1879, and part of the system from Le Cheylard to Lavoûte-sur-Loire, with a branch from Le Cheylard running north-east to Tournon by the River Rhone. Construction started in 1890 with sections being joined up in 1902/3, and the narrow-gauge secondary system completed from Yssingeaux eastward to Dunieres, where it terminated at the PLM (later SNCF) standard-gauge line from Roane in the north via Annonay to Serrieres, where it joined the north-south main line south to Lyon. These narrow gauge lines were modernised in the early 1930s and remained mostly in use until 1968, although closures of sections began in 1952 under the pressure of increasing road transport.

At that time the Vivrais, like most other secondary railways, relied on diesel railcars to maintain a passenger service, while the freight work was handled by Swiss-built Mallet 0-6-6-0 tank engines, which were able to tackle the severe gradient of 1 in 32 from Le Cheylard northward up to St Agreve on the branch to Dunieres. By 1969 service on this section had become erratic, but some improvements in the 1990s included the use of diesel locomotives. St Agreve was the main workshops and depot of the Vivrais at this time.

The Vivrais network consisted of 120 miles, operating in the Ardeche region. By the mid-1970s all the secondary narrow-gauge lines had closed commercially, but their presence can still be seen in many areas where great engineering features such as viaducts span deep gorges.

The Vivrais was partly revived with a 33km route from Tournon on the River Rhone to Lamastre, winding up the Le Doux River valley. At Tournon the Vivrais had its station back-to-back with the SNCF station and, on leaving, it joined and ran over dual-gauge track for about half a mile (0.8km) before leaving the main line for its climb up to Lamastre. Today

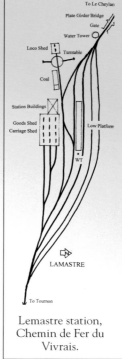

Lemastre station, Chemin de Fer du Vivrais.

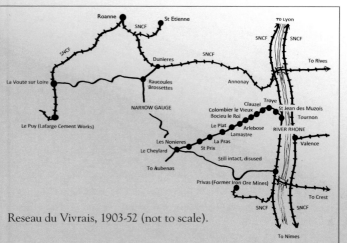

Reseau du Vivrais, 1903-52 (not to scale).

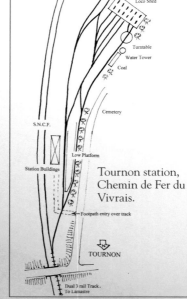

Tournon station, Chemin de Fer du Vivrais.

Pinguilet No 240 was built in 1909 and named *Isere*. This 'push-me-pull-you' 0-6-0 tank locomotive has a cab at each end, probably unique for a steam engine.

it can no longer run dual gauge over SNCF metals, so a new terminus complex has been constructed at St Jean des Muzols, which was the first halt after leaving the dual gauge from Tournon.

It is of 600mm gauge and has become a 'Touristiques' line run by 15 employees and some volunteers. Several locos and rolling stock were acquired from the Reseau Breton, probably in its day the most special secondary railway system in France.

The trip is spectacular, passing grape vines, rattling over level crossings and running through small halts. Entering a gorge known as Doux-Plage, there is a single-span bridge over the River Le Doux built in 1583, at one time the largest arched bridge in the world, and all this in the wilds of the Ardeche!

Mallet 0-6-6-0 tank locomotive No 4, built in 1932 by Sacu Graffenstaden, takes water at Boucieu-le-Roi, overlooked by a monastery atop a hill.

Above the station at Boucieu-le-Roi is the Chateau de Chazotte, which looks down on the hive of activity when the train stops to allow the locomotive to fill up with water. Clearly the French passengers were well aware of what was in store, but not so the tourists. On the broad platform area stood a number of stalls selling every conceivable type of local cheese, meat and wine. This was a lengthy stop for the 'gastronomes' to indulge themselves with considerable gusto! A

sharp 'toot' and the train left, leaving the station deserted! Further along the line a sign announced 'You are crossing the 45th parallel'. 'So what?' you may ask, but this is the point equidistant between the North Pole and the Equator. Evidently it was also the imaginary boundary between the Catholics to the north, who cook with butter, and the Protestants to the south, who cook with oil! For the French, food is everything.

Left: The railways also had a diesel, No X, which was rebuilt at Le Cheylard Works, further inland, from an 1897 0-6-2 steam locomotive.

Right: 0-6-6-0T Mallet No 414, with its unusual brown livery, stands in Lamastre yard ready to take its passengers to Tournon.

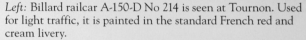

Left: Billard railcar A-150-D No 214 is seen at Tournon. Used for light traffic, it is painted in the standard French red and cream livery.

The train is timed to arrive at Lamastre by lunchtime and the passengers disperse around the small town for food and wine. Meanwhile the loco is fed and watered, then turned on the turntable ready for the trip back to Tournon. The line once continued over an old steel truss bridge crossing a stream towards Le Cheylard, but there is now just a short headshunt continuing into long grass with several rusty wagons gradually falling apart. There are several sidings opposite the station and an old carriage shed housing a couple of defunct railcars.

The Vivrais closed on 13 April 2008 through lack of funds, but after an injection of cash steam ran again in July 2013, albeit over just 10 miles (16km). One Mallet

locomotive is in use, with a second being overhauled with a view to a more regular and permanent service in the future.

However, the future at the time of writing still looks uncertain indeed, especially in these times of financial restraint, but problems are challenges that can be surmounted with good will all round.

Above: In the loco shed yard at Tournon is Mallet No 403, built in 1903; note the long throw of the piston rod and the two decorative lamps, as well as the small rail trolley and jack in the foreground.

Above right: An early-morning general view of Tournon engine shed, with the Billard railcar in front of the coach sidings on the extreme left and three locomotives in steam on the right.

Right: Boucieu-le-Roi provides water for the locomotives, and for the passengers a shopping treat of local products. C'est magnifique!

Le Chemin de Fer de la Baie de Somme

Le Chemin de Fer de la Baie de Somme (Somme Bay Railway) is a delightful single-track, metre-gauge (3ft 3 in) heritage light railway running around the bay where the River Somme flows into the English Channel, approximately 105km (65 miles) south of Calais.

The terminus at the northern end of the line is Le Crotoy, a small seaside town with a sandy beach on the estuary. The terminus on the southern side of the bay is St-Valery, situated at the point where the river enters the bay. The track loops around the bay on an embankment and replaces an early wooden trestle bridge structure. St-Valery boasts two stations, St-Valery Ville (Town) and St-Valery Quai (Quayside); the latter is the terminus, and locomotives are turned on an electric turntable.

St-Valery Ville is where a 12km line diverges off in a

Edition de l'Hôtel des Voyageurs

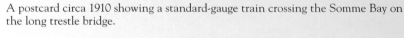

A postcard circa 1910 showing a standard-gauge train crossing the Somme Bay on the long trestle bridge.

westerly direction to Cayeux-Brighton Plage, exposed to the Channel coast and sitting behind a wall of sea pebbles. Between St-Valery and Le Crotoy is Noyelles station, where interchange is available with the standard-gauge SNCF Calais and Abbeville line. The line from Noyelles to St-Valery has dual gauge, with the metre gauge laid inside the standard gauge (four rails) from Noyelles, converting to three-rail dual gauge at St-Valery, with one rail being common to both gauges.

A view looking down the River Somme to St-Valery Quai, where a turntable is available to turn the locomotives. On the right is a veranda coach BDF 26 from the former Chemin de Fer Yverdon-Ste-Croix, built in 1893; note the dual standard- and metre-gauge track it is standing on.

Left: A train leaves St-Valery Ville station for Le Crotoy, round the other side of the bay. The locomotive is 2-6-0T No 15, built in 1920 by Haine-Saint-Pierre Foundries, Belgium, works No 1316.

Above: No 15's builder's plate.

The dual-gauge line gives the opportunity for standard-gauge locomotives to visit the line. This is done periodically through the Somme Bay Railway's twinning with the Kent & East Sussex Railway, being the nearest English heritage railway to the French coast.

History

Planning, owning and running railways in France has always been a government responsibility, split into major and minor routes, regions and gauges. This line has a long and complex history.

The original 5.6km (3½-mile) standard-gauge line was opened in 1858 and connected Noyelles to St-Valery by a long 1,367m (1,945-yard) wooden trestle bridge over the Somme Bay; this bridge was replaced by an embankment in 1912. A lift bridge over the Somme Canal was installed to allow shipping to enter and leave. A station was built on the St-Valery side of the canal and became St-Valery Canal Halt, although it was some distance from the town. The journey time in each direction between Noyelles and St-Valery was 12 minutes.

In July 1887 7.5km (4.7 miles) of metre-gauge line was opened from Noyelles to Le Crotoy, and 18km (11 miles) from Noyelles to Cayeux in September of that year; the metre-gauge line was laid between the standard gauge rails and extended into St-Valery Ville.

This little steam railway, operated by 0-6-2 tank locomotives, carried regular passengers and holidaymakers in the summer to the resorts around the bay area, and small stations and halts were opened to accommodate them.

Various goods were also transported, including sugar beet, chicory, shellfish and flint pebbles (galets); the latter were used in the ceramics industry. Most of the locomotives were fitted with twin sets of buffers, the centre pair for the metre-gauge wagons and the outer pair for standard-gauge stock.

These three metre-gauge lines, together with two others in the Somme region, became 'Reseau des Bains de Mer' (loosely translated as the 'sea bathing network') and was part of the Chemins de Fer Département de la Somme (the Somme Railway Department). This network consisted of some 340km (212 miles) of track, of which Reseau des Bains de Mer accounted for only 25.5km (16 miles).

Being located on the west coast and on the estuary of the River Somme, the area became occupied by both Allied and invading armies in the Franco Prussian War (1870-73), and by the German Army during both World Wars. The little railway was requisitioned for war work, but survived the ordeal.

After the Second World War the 0-6-2 tank locomotives continued to haul around 40,000 tons of sugar beet to the local processing plant at Lancheres, 10,000 tons of galets, and of course passengers. But by the late 1960s all traffic had declined and all three narrow-gauge lines were closed. SNCF continued to use the standard-gauge tracks from Noyelles to St-Valery for occasional freight haulage, but this was eventually closed to traffic from 1 January 1993.

Veranda coach No BCF10502, 2nd and 3rd Class, was built by Manage of Belgium in 1920.

Preservation of the three lines

A preservation group was set up in November 1969 to reopen the Noyelles-Le Crotoy line to tourists, and in March 1970 became Chemin de Fer de la Baie de Somme (CFBS). After the Cayeux line closed CFBS set up a separate company to reopen it between Noyelles and Cayeux and run the trains, but was unsuccessful in taking over the Noyelles-St-Valery standard-gauge freight business from SNCF.

In 1982 CFBS became the preservation group for all three Somme Bay lines. The St-Valery to Cayeux line is only operated during summer months.

Unfortunately, none of the original 0-6-2 tank locomotives of the Reseau des Bains de Mer era survived into preservation. However, out of the CFBS's stock of 10 steam locomotives, the Haine-Saint-Pierre 2-6-0T No 1316, built in 1920, is the most representative of the group. It was built at the same time as Nos 1304-14, four of which worked on the line.

The stock list also contains six diesel locomotives, one of which is standard gauge, six railcars, coaches and wagons.

The Somme Bay area is a uniquely beautiful place to visit and St-Valery is everything a small French coastal town should be, with plenty of character, excellent seafood and of course the railway.

France: Railways of the South

Left: The beautiful Chateau Monbazillac perched on a hill overlooking Bergerac, surrounded by grape vines. Monbazillac dessert wines are some of the best in France..

Right: A Class 81500, No.81830 built by Bombardier between 2004 and 2007 for SNCF as a dual EMU/ DMU. Electrical supply is 1.5KV DC collected via pantograph. Seen here at Le Buisson-de-Cadouin approximately 20 miles (32km) from Sarlat.

Right: The red and white square signal panels at the ends of the platforms at Le Buisson. Face on means STOP and edge on CLEAR.

Dordogne River Valley line

This picturesque secondary line runs between Bordeaux-St-Jean and Sarlat-la-Caneda in the Aquitaine region of south-west France, and runs due east alongside the Dordogne River, passing through villages, towns and dense woodland and over several river bridges. The route is 122 miles (195km) long with up to six *slow* trains per day each way, affording plenty of time to enjoy the scenery!

The line to Sarlat was opened between 1875 and 1882 by the Compagnie du Chemin de Fer de Paris à Orleans, from Bordeaux, linking the medieval wine towns of St-Emilion and Bergerac, then on to Le Buisson-de-Cadouin and Sarlat.

The single track with passing loops at stations is not electrified, and steam eventually gave way to diesel power. Today modern regional diesel multiple units (DMUs) provide a comfortable air-conditioned journey.

Signalling along the line is still mainly mechanical, using interlocking lever frames. The mechanical signals consist of a red and white square board on a post; when face-on to the train the board means 'absolute stop', while turned edge-on signifies a 'clear' signal.

The stations at Bergerac and Le Buisson have many sidings, now unused, with little or no sign of wagons or coaches. Goods sheds and locomotive sheds have been put to other uses and there is gradual decay, with grass and vegetation beginning to take hold. Even so, the now rustic nature of these areas still has its attractions.

Above: DMU Class 72500, No.72593/4 built by Alstom between 1997 and 2002 for SNCF and on the left a Class 2200 DMU, No. 2212, built by ANF between 1985 and 1988 and normally stabled at Bordeaux St Jean. Seen here at Bergerac Station when trains were halted by a derailment.

Right: A postcard from the early 1900's of the entrance to St Juery Steelworks clearly showing the railway lines.

Far right: One of the portals of Vassiere tunnel, 440 metres in length, built in 1920.

The railway that never was

In the Midi-Pyrenees area of France is the attractive town of Albi, situated on the banks of the River Tarn. Leaving Albi in an easterly direction, the road soon arrives in St-Juery and follows the rugged river valley in the direction of Millau.

It soon becomes apparent that the road was once a railway track – man-made embankments, gentle curves, standardised railway iron railings on small bridges, a virtually flat gradient and surprisingly tunnels through rocky outcrops. Driving further through the Tarn valley some very attractive bridges have been built over the river to overcome the constant meandering, thus avoiding too much tunnelling and to accommodate villages along the way. Most of the tunnels and bridges form part of the local D-road system along the valley.

So, the question arises, where did the railway go to and when and why did it cease to operate? Further investigation revealed that it was a standard-gauge line to run from Albi via St-Juery, terminating at a small town to the east called St-Affrique; it was declared to be a public utility on 20 June 1881.

In 1883 the concession was awarded to the Midi Railway Company, together with a neighbouring line from Tournemire (Roquefort) to Le Vigan (see below). The Vigan line opened as early as 1896, but it was not until 1904 that construction started on the 73km (45.6-mile) St-Affrique to St-Juery section, although the 9km (5.6-mile) Albi to St-Juery section had opened in 1899, mainly due to the insistence and tenacity of the St-Juery steelworks, which required the line for the expansion of its business. The line also carried passengers.

Work on the St-Affrique to St-Juery section was carried out using mainly foreign workers. During the First World War the work was

The rail bridge at Girbes now a part of the drive through the Tarn Valley to St Affrique, Roquefort and Millau.

obviously spasmodic, but construction continued using German prisoners of war, then continued in earnest in the 1920s.

By 1932 the Midi Company had built eight bridges over the Tarn and excavated 18 tunnels, but stated its reluctance to finish construction due to economic conditions. Two years later the company obtained official authorisation to stop further work, such as laying track and installing signalling, until conditions improved. Progress along the route can be judged from the dates on the keystones above tunnel entrances, which range from 1914 to 1928.

In 1938 SNCF was created and the viability of smaller lines came under scrutiny. It was decided that the St-Affrique to St-Juery line would never be completed, and the line was officially decommissioned on 30 November 1941.

The Albi-St Juery section continued in service, but ceased to carry passengers in 1933,

and closed to freight in 1983 when the steelworks went out of business. The line was officially closed in 2001, although some of the track is still there and gradually being taken over by nature.

St-Affrique-Tournemire (Roquefort)-Le Vigan

A short branch was opened between St-Affrique and Tournemire in 1896 in preparation for the Albi-St Juery line to join it. The line from St-Affrique joined the main north-south Beziers-Neussarques line for a short distance south of Tournemire, then branched east towards Le Vigan just north of the station.

Typical locomotives used at the time were Midi Railway tender 0-6-0s (030s in France) of Type 030TD, manufactured by Schneider between 1883 and 1886. It must be assumed

A postcard dated around 1900 of St-Affrique station showing an 0-6-0 with tender waiting to depart for Tournemire.

that if the St-Affrique to St-Juery line had been completed, this type of locomotive or similar would have been the motive power mainstay.

In 1938 passenger traffic ceased and there was freight only on the branch until 1991, when the line was closed; it was decommissioned in 2000.

The main line: Beziers-Neussarques

Tournemire station in the early 1900s was a busy place with a large canopy over the platforms. Locomotives employed on the main line were mainly Midi 4-6-0 (230 in France) '1314s', built in 1902 by SACM Belfort for this line. They were a German design developed for the Black Forest. Today Tournemire is just a country station, and most trains pass straight through.

A postcard showing Tournemire station at its peak in the first few years of the 20th century. A Midi 4-6-0 (230 in France) is proudly displayed for the camera.

Corsica

The Mediterranean island of Corsica is part of France and enjoys a railway system that reflects its national identity. Located off the French and Italian coasts, its Italian neighbour, the island of Sardinia, is just 7.7 miles (12.25km) off its southern tip.

Bastia, situated in the north-east, is Corsica's capital, with the railway headquarters and workshops at Casamoza, just to the south. A rail junction here had a line running due south almost the length of the island, following closely the east coast down to the small port of Porto-Vecchio. The other line heads west into the hilly countryside, arriving at the port of Ajaccio after a tortuous journey. From Ponte Leccia another branch heads north to the coast, then descends and turns west, passing through the port of Ile Rousse then, almost on the seashore, terminating at the sea ferry port of Calvi. Construction work commenced on the Bastia-Ajaccio line, a distance of 157km, from the two ends, both with considerable engineering problems, joining up in 1894.

By 1914 the island's network extended to 295km, but during the Second World War, despite the island being within the Free French territory, it was occupied by the Germans. During their retreat, much damage was caused to the eastern branch to Porto-Vecchio, and it never reopened.

This Corsican Railways 0-6-2T was one of 14 built by Fives-Lille between 1887 and 1888. It is portrayed shunting at the southern port of Ajaccio. *Ian Peaty*

Bastia-Ajaccio

A driver's-eye view from a railcar heading for Ajaccio on the south coast, crossing the superb viaduct built by Gustav Eiffel, of Paris tower fame, and heading into the mountains covered in chestnut trees.

Ponte Leccia is a small town in the centre of the island with a very typical French rural station with low island platforms, a few sidings and an old engine shed. With its central position on the line, a permanent way service vehicle is based here with several open wagons for ballast, etc. One of the two Geismar vehicles, No 850.02, has a platform crane and is liveried in blue and white, the colours of SNCF (CFC).

The track from Bastia, which once included a branch down to the docks, was remodelled in the 1980s with a new station building and the tracks going through the La Torreto Tunnel (1,442 metres) under the town. From Casamoza Junction to Ponte Leccia is 46km, with five tunnels and several impressive bridges along the way. The main line on to Ajaccio is also spectacular, as it twists and turns climbing into the chestnut-clad hills for which Corsica is famous (even the excellent local beer, Pietra, is made with chestnuts!).

More or less mid-way to Ajaccio is the university town of Corte, high up in the hills. From there heading south the line passes through 11 tunnels and over two major viaducts. For 17km the gradient is 1 in 33, during which the line takes a spectacular 8km winding course from one river valley to another, passing through Vivario. The Pont du Vecchio viaduct was designed by Gustav Eiffel, of Paris tower fame; it is 94 metres high and 140 metres long, and has two stone-

built arches at each end with two slim columns supporting three metal truss beams. The central portion spans the old road bridge, which is integral to the overall design, and was completed on 10 October 1892.

Gradients down towards Ajaccio from this summit and watershed vary from 1 in 40 to 1 in 50 to Mezzana, where the line eases out for the final 15km to the port. Mediterranean cruise ships call at Ajaccio, with many passengers sampling the local speciality of herbal oils and

scents, made from the 'Maquis' vegetation.

This Bastia-Ajaccio line is metre gauge, and still carries freight, although of a meagre nature. Diesel locos are of the Bo-Bo type, hydro-mechanical CFD Montmirail. No 404, built in 1963, is ex-CFD Provence of 1974; two other similar ones are No 405 of 1966 and No 406 of 1973, all of 400hp. No 404 has lightweight frames, so carries additional weights on each side to improve adhesion.

In 2012 a Soule railcar and trailer arrive at the junction station of Ponte Leccia from Bastia for the onward journey to Ajaccio.

Ponte Leccia-Calvi

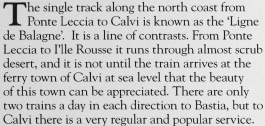

The single track along the north coast from Ponte Leccia to Calvi is known as the 'Ligne de Balagne'. It is a line of contrasts. From Ponte Leccia to I'lle Rousse it runs through almost scrub desert, and it is not until the train arrives at the ferry town of Calvi at sea level that the beauty of this town can be appreciated. There are only two trains a day in each direction to Bastia, but to Calvi there is a very regular and popular service.

The track hugs the rocky coast with its many small beaches and lovely views, with the train stopping at the pretty town of Algajola, complete with its own castle on the shore. Calanzana Lumio's station serves the French Foreign Legion military base and it is here that the narrow-gauge track rapidly passes over three metal truss bridges crossing boulder-strewn rivers from the mountains inland. On the approach to Calvi the line runs along the beaches, where the track is almost hidden by the white sand, which drifts into the pine woods. As the line curves into the town's station, several sidings and loops indicate its former importance, as do the remains of a three-stall roundhouse for locomotives. Only five years ago the traditional red and cream livery of French railcars was to be seen, but now slim-line silver and blue railcars provide an excellent and most enjoyable service to I'lle Rousse and back.

The older railcars were by Billard, Type A150D built in 1937, A150 D6 from the same year, and Type A210D from 1935/6, all liveried in red and

Twin-car unit CFD X2005 with trailer X2001, in white and blue livery, leaves Ponte Leccia for Calvi. The junction is a short distance away to the north.

cream. Renault autorails Nos ABH 6 and 8 were built in 1949/50. The present modern stock in the silver and blue livery was built by Soule in 1989/92 in Series 55, the later Series 57 being built in 1997. These are worked in multiple units, some with older trailer cars.

Calvi is the jewel in the crown of Corsica. It has a harbour for pleasure ships as well as serving a commercial vehicle ferry, which connects the island with mainland France and Sardinia. The port area has numerous restaurants on the quayside, which is overlooked by the castle on a high mount.

The branch was considered for closure in

1955 due to two-thirds of the line producing very little revenue, as it passed through a sparsely populated mountainous area. However, both rail workers and islanders fought to retain the line, with the result that the operators handed it over to the Government in 1983. It was then run by SNCF, which invested in the infrastructure to the tune of 110 million euros, enabling the new rolling stock to be acquired.

Right: An old red and cream liveried Renault railcar hauling a Billard trailer unit built in 1938 calls at the typical wayside station at Algajola.

Below: Calvi's terminus station has an engine shed and a few sidings, with a rebodied railcar used for lightweight freight and packages.

Below right: With sun-worshippers, a sandy beach and pine woods beside Calvi Bay, a railcar approaches the French Foreign Legion base on its way to the inland junction at Ponte Leccia.

A railcar from Ponte Leccia approaches a passing loop on the return journey to Calvi, with a single Renault railcar on the left.

Portugal

Portugal, in south-west of Europe, has its western side bordering the Atlantic Ocean and its remaining sides surrounded by Spain. It is relatively small in area and population when compared with its Spanish neighbour, and is split across by two rivers that flow from Spain: the Tagus, which meets the sea at Lisbon, and the Douro, at Oporto (Porto to the Portuguese, the town that gave its name to the country). The majority of the population live along the western coastal areas; Lisbon, in the south, is the largest city, followed by Oporto in the north. Inland, most of

The spectacular Lisbon Orient station, opened in 1998 for the Expo '98 World Fair, is the main transport hub in the capital. There are six platforms used by the 'Alfa Pendular', international, regional express and commuter services.

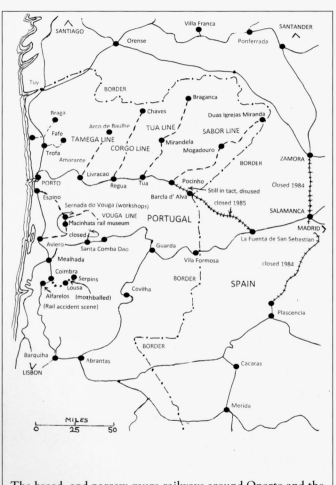

The broad- and narrow-gauge railways around Oporto and the Douro Valley, Portugal.

A Lisbon suburban broad-gauge train, CP Class 2300 No 2386, arrives at Lisbon Orient. Built by a Siemens/Bombardier consortium between 1992 and 1996, they are four-car 25kV AC EMU sets powered from the overhead catenary.

A metre-gauge Class 9630 DMU slices through nature as it approaches Agueda. These two-coach units were built in Portugal by Sorefame and entered service in 1991.

the countryside is given over to agriculture with a profusion of vineyards, especially in the Douro region. The most southerly region around the Algarve plays host to countless sun-seeking holidaymakers.

Portugal is roughly rectangular, measuring about 575km from north to south by 210km across (357 by 130 miles), which means that it is about three times longer than its width. Therefore most of the fast railway lines run north-south, serving Lisbon, Coimbra, Aviero, Vila Nova de Gaia and Oporto, with local branch lines serving the hinterland.

The Portuguese rail network, Comboios de Portugal (CP – Trains of Portugal), is a

state-owned company founded in 1951. The normal running gauge is a 'broad' gauge of 1,668mm (5ft 5 in), with a total track length of 2,603km (1,617 miles), of which 1,351km (839 miles) is electrified with a 25kV/50Hz AC overhead catenary system. There is a short 25km (16-mile) stretch of 1,500V DC on the Cascais line out of Lisbon.

Last, but not least, are the narrow, metre-gauge lines in the north around the Oporto region. Sadly, only the Linha da Vouga line remains open, but the NG network still has plenty to offer to stir memories of times gone by.

A busy moment at Agueda. The stations are used as the passing places along this single track.

The Vouga line

The 97km (60-mile) narrow-gauge Linha da Vouga serves the country region between Oporto and Coimbra. It was opened in 1910 with its northern terminus at Espinho, where it meets the Oporto-Coimbra-Lisbon broad-gauge main line; it then runs southwards inland on an almost circular route, eventually joining up with the main line again at Aviero. Another 79km (49-mile) branch was opened in 1914 from Sernada do Vouga westwards to Viseu, but this was closed in 1990.

The narrow-gauge steam locomotives used were 2-4-6-0 Mallets, 2-8-2Ts and 2-6-0Ts. However, steam started to be phased out as early as the 1940s in favour of six-cylinder diesel railcars constructed at the railway's Sernada workshops using components from old Panhard buses. Nonetheless steam held on until the 1970s, when it was finally replaced by Dutch-built Series 9300 railcars. Since 2002 services on the line have been largely operated by seven of CP's Series 9630 two-car DMUs made by Sorefame in 1991, and originally used on the Oporto narrow-gauge lines out of Trindade until replaced by the new Metro network.

The Sernada workshop is still maintaining the current DMUs and removing the 'spray-can menace' that seems to affect most units, but the surrounding yard and sidings area with its turntable has been left to nature to decide its future. However, it is still well worth a visit to soak up the atmosphere!

The whole line has that 'slipping into dereliction' look, while at the same time presenting itself as a quaint and unique operation that takes the visitor through some outstanding countryside and 'time warp' villages. As the line leaves Sernada in the direction of Macinhata it traverses an impressive masonry viaduct over the Vouga River. The track is set across the middle of the roadway with warning lights at each end for

Ex-CP 'E123' 4-6-0T locomotive, formerly No VV313, was built in 1908 by Borsig for the Vale do Vouga Railway, and is now on display at the Macinhata do Vouga Railway Museum near Agueda.

Small and novel, locally used metre-gauge diesel railcar No DIF/VIA DIE-3, in striking yellow paintwork, is also on display at the Macinhata museum.

the infrequent local traffic. In the goods yard at Macinhata do Vouga station is a railway museum, which houses a remarkable collection of steam locomotives, railcars, rolling stock and memorabilia from that bygone age, well presented and deserving a visit.

Unfortunately, this last narrow-gauge line is under threat of closure in the near future and a worthy tourist attraction could sadly disappear.

Above: The museum's CP metre-gauge diesel railcar No NE-51 has a more streamlined design, similar to that of a road coach of the time.

Above right: This original blue and white tiled picture illustrates a Vouga line steam locomotive pulling a train across a masonry viaduct over the River Vouga, circa 1910.

Right: Seen at Sernada do Vouga station and workshops are a Henschel 2-8-2T on the right and a Kessler 0-6-0T on the left. The viaduct to the left is shared with road and rail. *Ian Peaty*

The yard at Sernada do Vouga in more recent times, clearly depicting an atmosphere of dereliction.
All the Class 9630 units have been on the receiving end of the local graffiti artists.

Oporto

Oporto is a World Heritage Site and is situated on the north bank of the Douro River. The city has two main stations, Campanha, which is the main through station for non-local and inter-city trains, and Sao Bento, which sits serenely in Almeida Square in the middle of the city. It was opened in 1916 and serves local broad-gauge lines going north, and is the western terminus for the Douro Valley line, which follows the river towards the Spanish border. The station is famous for its tiled panels in the main concourse depicting various events in Portugal's history.

The trains operating the suburban lines are four-car EMUs of Class 3400, built by Bombardier in 2005 with a top speed of 140km/h (87mph) and powered by a 25kV/50Hz overhead catenary system.

A Vouga line sign: 'Stop, Look and Listen. For Pedestrian use only.'

Inside the main concourse of Sao Bento station, in the middle of Oporto, showing its famous tiled panels depicting Portugal's history.
Sao Bento serves the local broad-gauge lines and is the terminus for the Douro Valley line.

A Bombardier-built Class 3400 broad-gauge four-car EMU emerges from the tunnel into Oporto station. These are the mainstay of the local network and have been entering service since 2005.

The Douro line

A broad-gauge mixed train is seen in the Douro Valley with the hills covered in grapevines. This line formerly connected within the Spanish railway network at the Portuguese-Spanish border at Barca d'Alva. *Ian Peaty*

This broad gauge line is not electrified and requires the use of DMUs. These are Spanish RENFE three-car sets built in the early 1980s with a top speed of 120km/h (75mph). They are classed as 'C592' and are on lease from RENFE. They have replaced the Portuguese Sorefame, stainless-steel, three-car 600 Series, which were originally introduced in batches from 1979. The carriage design and build was that of the Budd Company in the USA, and they were built under licence at Sorefame's Amadora factory.

Seven original broad-gauge steam locomotives that served the Douro line have been left to nature at the far side of the freight yard at Vila Nova de Gaia, the station on the south side of the Douro River; they make a sad but tranquil sight with the electric-blue flowering convolvulus and golden honeysuckle hiding their rusting shells. They are a mixture of 2-8-0, 4-6-0 and 2-8-4T locomotives that were retired in the 1970s.

Leaving Oporto, the single-track, broad-

gauge line turns inland away from the River Douro, then curves back again and joins it on the north bank at Pala, about 75km (47 miles) from Oporto. The line then follows the river, arriving at small towns on the way, clinging to the side of sheer cliffs, passing through granite tunnels, over attractive bridges, and at times being only a few feet higher than the river level. The Douro line has 26 tunnels and 30 bridges, and not only connects the small towns and villages along the riverside, but also once connected with the termini of the narrow-gauge lines that puffed and wheezed their way up into the hills beyond.

The line also serves Regua, a small town on the river approximately 103km (64 miles) from Oporto by rail, and also the terminus of the former narrow-gauge Corgo line. It was an important centre for the port wine trade when growers relied on the 'little trains' to transport the grapes from the villages in the hills. The station and yard area is quite expansive, but now that the Corgo line is closed there is little activity apart from the 12 daily Douro line trains in each direction.

Pinhao is another 23.4km (14.6 miles) further east and is a small, attractive, traditional town on the riverside surrounded by vine-covered hillsides. Its station deserves a mention, as it is clad in the traditional Portuguese blue and white tiles depicting the Douro and other local scenes. Even the toilets have their fair share of blue tiles!

A further 13km (8.1 miles) brings us to Tua, which was the terminus of the now closed narrow-gauge Tua line.

From Tua the Douro line crosses the river at Ferradosa by a new bridge built in 1980. It is 375 metres (410 yards) long and replaced the original bridge that opened in 1887 and crossed the river about 1km (⅝ mile) downstream; when the Valeira Dam was built in 1975 the river level gradually rose behind it to a height that made navigation under the bridge impossible, so it was dismantled and the new one built. The remaining bridge buttresses are clear to see on each side of the river. The line was then extended along a

A Spanish RENFE Class C592 three-car DMU travels along the single-track broad-gauge line between Oporto and Pocinho, the terminus of the line today. This is a stunning journey along the side of the river with rugged scenery and vineyards galore!

straight 300-metre (330-yard) concrete platform, specially built, on the side of the north bank, as the shoreline contours would not be suitable for broad-gauge track. The line then rejoins the north bank before the new bridge, which is set at a favourable angle across the river to facilitate an easy curve onto it. The line then continues to its eastern terminus at Pocinho, about 171km (107 miles) from Oporto. Pocinho was also the terminus for the narrow-gauge Sabor line, which

closed completely in 1988.

The original terminus for the Douro line was at Barca d'Alva on the Portuguese-Spanish border. The 28km (17½-mile) line from Pocinho to Barca d'Alva was officially opened in December 1887 together with the broad-gauge line from Salamanca in Spain. The buffers of the Portuguese and Spanish steam locomotives 'kissed' in the middle of the international rail bridge over the River Agueda, a tributary of the

Douro, and the opening ceremony was completed. Apart from the important commercial traffic, the 135km (84-mile) route from Barca d'Alva through to Salamanca was used by international passengers destined for cities like Madrid and Paris. Eventually railcars took over from steam locomotives to ensure that passengers were given a quicker and more reliable service from Oporto to meet the Spanish train waiting at Barca d'Alva. The Spanish rail company, RENFE, closed the line to Salamanca in 1985 for economic reasons, and the line from Pocinho to Barca d'Alva was closed on the Portuguese side in May 1988.

Today at Barca d'Alva the track, station and bridges are still there, despite the march of nature that appears to be slowly claiming the railway as its own. The track is in a bad state of decay with the wooden sleepers falling apart. The decay is so advanced that the screw spikes securing the flanges of the flat-bottom rails to the sleepers can be pulled out by hand. The station was also the border control and included offices for immigration, customs, international telegraph, etc, and is quite a large imposing building.

This is a typical example of bridge architecture along the Douro. There are many inlets and small rivers flowing into the river that must be crossed by the railway.

Above: This 'special' at Pocinho terminus has CP Class 1400 diesel No 1411 at the business end. The engines were designed and engineered by English Electric; the first ten were built at the Vulcan Foundry, with the remaining 57 assembled by Sorefame in Portugal between 1967 and 1969.

Right: The station at Barca d'Alva, closed since 1988, is being overrun by nature, although the track is still visible in the foreground. It is an imposing building that was not only the terminus of the Douro line but served as the administrative border for the continuing rail link to Salamanca in Spain.

Lower right: The three-road engine house still stands at Barca d'Alva, with a turntable for turning the typical 4-6-0 tender locomotives that hauled the trains from Oporto. These locomotives were mainly built by Henschel of Germany.

Left: This is a typical broad-gauge steam locomotive that once worked on the Douro Valley line, one of a number gradually decaying at the back of the yard at Vila Nova de Gaia. At least their resting place is a peaceful one.

The disused rail bridge over the River Agueda, a tributary of the Douro, was the border crossing between Portugal and Spain. The Spanish company RENFE closed the Salamanca link in 1985.

The goods shed is in reasonable condition and a three-road locomotive roundhouse with turntable is situated further along the track towards the international bridge. Some of the trackside telegraph poles are still standing with the insulators mounted on the side and wires hanging down and waving sadly in the breeze, a final acceptance of contact lost.

At this juncture it is worth noting that Spain and Portugal shared the same broad gauge, although their gauges were slightly different. The Spanish gauge was 1,672mm (5ft 5^{13}/$_{16}$in) and the Portuguese gauge was 1,664mm (5ft 5½in), a difference of 8mm (0.31in). In the early days this was not too much of a problem when crossing borders, as speeds were relatively slow, but as speeds and risks increased a compromise gauge was agreed

in 1955 at 1,668mm (5ft 5^{21}/$_{32}$ in), known as the 'Iberian gauge'. However, the high-speed lines of today in both Portugal and Spain have reverted to the standard gauge of 1,435mm (4ft 8½in) so that they can link with the rest of the European railway network.

Above top: The peaceful landscape downstream from Barca d'Alva will never hear the beat of the engine, smell the sulphur or see the smoke again.

Above: This velocipede was used on the Douro Valley line – hard work without gears!

Left: Another Douro line velocipede, this time a motorbike conversion.

The Douro narrow-gauge lines

The narrow-gauge lines that terminated along the Douro were metre gauge (1,000mm/3ft 3⅜in), and followed the rivers they were named after. They wound their way down from the villages in the hills to meet the broad-gauge Douro line at the river's edge. All these lines ran north from the Douro towards the Spanish border.

Sadly, as road networks improved greatly and village life changed, the viability of running small railways became uneconomic, resulting in closure of these lines, in part or completely, from the 1980s; they are now all closed apart from the Vouga line, which is not in the Douro area.

These metre-gauge lines were scenes of excitement and pleasure in the heyday of steam, as whole families, often of three generations, travelled from the small towns and villages in the hills, bringing their goods for sale to the larger towns along the Douro valley.

The Sabor line

The Sabor line ran from its southern terminus at Pocinho to its northern terminus at Duas Igrejas. As soon as it left Pocinho, on the south bank of the Douro, it curved left to cross a viaduct over the river and started its uphill climb towards Duas Igrejas.

Construction of the line started in 1904 and took many years, with the opening of the first section from Pocinho to Carvicais in 1911. The line was completed to its northern terminus in 1938, a total of 106km (66 miles), with 21 stations en route.

Freight and heavy mixed trains and iron ore were hauled almost exclusively by 2-6-4-0T Mallet steam locomotives, but after the iron ore traffic ceased in 1970 and the freight traffic declined, diesel locomotives were often used. Passengers were mostly transported by petrol or diesel railcars, then by local buses from the 1970s. The line closed in 1988.

The Tua line

The Tua line, 32km (20 miles) west of Pocinho, was the oldest and longest of the narrow-gauge lines along the Douro valley. The first section, of 55km (34 miles), opened from Tua town, on the Douro, to Mirandela in 1887. The line left Tua, a station it shared with the broad gauge Douro line, in a westerly direction towards Regua and almost immediately curved to the north and climbed up the steeply graded line along the gorge of the River Tua towards Mirandela.

The line was then extended another 79km (49 miles) in 1906 to the northerly town of Braganca, close to the Spanish border. At one time an extension over the border into Spain was envisaged, but this failed to materialise.

Top right: A broad-gauge 2-8-4T locomotive at Tua taking water during a special tour. Built by Henschel in 1924, it is CFP No 0186. Note the extra water wagon and the large, elderly luggage van behind.

Mirandela became the operating headquarters, with 40 stations and halts along the whole line.

The steam locomotives that served the line until the mid-1970s were 0-4-4-0T Mallets, 2-6-0Ts and 0-6-0Ts, then as steam was phased out trains were hauled by CP Class 9020 diesels, and passenger services were frequently operated using Dutch diesel railcars (Allen of Rotterdam). As time went by new Series 9300 and 9500 diesel railcars took over the passenger traffic.

The whole line continued to operate until 1992, when the northern section from Mirandela to Braganca was formerly closed for economic reasons. The southern section,

Above: Three Series 9500 railcars are seen at Mirandela on the Tua narrow-gauge line. Although the line was closed in 2008, a short Metro line operates around the Mirandela area.

between Mirandela and Tua, continued to provide a service until 2008, when the derailment of a railcar near Brunheda, about 21km (13 miles) north of Tua, closed the line. The derailment caused the death of one passenger and injured 25 others. Repair of the track was difficult to undertake as at that point it was suspended on girders set in the side of the rock face. Consequently the line was never reopened, and closed formally in 2008.

However, a short Metro line continues to operate around Mirandela (Metro de Mirandela) using two Series 9500 railcars.

The Corgo line

The Corgo line, of metre gauge, 36.5km (23 miles) west of Tua, shared its terminus with the Douro broad-gauge line station at Regua and was probably the busiest narrow-gauge railway along the Douro Valley. The line left Regua in an easterly direction towards Tua, then immediately curved left, away from the Douro, and started its climb northwards along the gorge of the River Corgo.

The first section of 25km (16½ miles) between Regua and Vila Real, one of the principal towns in the area, was opened in 1906, with the remaining 71km (44 miles) opening in stages from 1907 to the northern terminus at Chaves in 1921, on a plateau just a few miles from the Spanish border. In common with all the narrow-gauge lines, the nearer they got to the River Douro the busier they became, and the Corgo line was no exception, the section

Below: In the disused yard at Regua several metre-gauge 2-4-6-0T Mallets built by Henschel are gradually rusting away, their work completed. They were ideal locomotives for the heavily graded stretches of the narrow-gauge lines.

Above: This delightful little metre-gauge locomotive is No E1, an 0-4-0T built by Henschel in 1922. It was then bought second-hand in 1943 and spent the rest of its days as a shunter around Regua yard. It is now on permanent display opposite the station platform.

Left: This is a better example of a narrow-gauge Mallet, taken a few years earlier at Regua, showing all its moving parts.

from Vila Real to Regua providing the majority of the railway's income.

So it was probably no surprise when the northern part of the line from Vila Real to Chaves closed in 1990. The line from Vila Real to Regua managed to survive until 2009, when the service was suspended pending urgent repairs to the track. Due to lack of funds these repairs have not been carried out and the line remains closed.

From the line's opening until the 1970s the trains were steam-hauled by 2-4-6-0T Mallets built by Henschel, which were ideal for the heavily graded southern section of the line. Since closure a collection of Mallets used on the Corgo and the other narrow-gauge lines have been left to nature in their own locomotive graveyard on the far side of the station yard at Regua.

Today, everything remains as it was except that there are no narrow-gauge trains, most of the sidings are devoid of rolling stock, and the dual-gauge turntable sits waiting to turn another broad- or narrow-gauge steam locomotive, while the remaining rusting Mallets look mournfully from their resting place.

The Tamega line

The Tamega line, 48km (30 miles) west of Regua, was the last narrow-gauge line to be encountered before reaching Oporto. At Mosteiro the Douro broad-gauge line swings inland away from the river and the Tamega narrow-gauge line meets it at Livracao station, its southern terminus.

The line stretches for 51.6km (32 miles) from Livracao to its northern terminus of Arco de Baulhe, with a total of 18 stations. The first 12.8km (8-mile) section of line to open, with all the attendant pomp and ceremony, was from

This is Livracao, the southern terminus of the now-closed Tamega narrow-gauge line. It was also the interchange for the broad-gauge Douro line that runs through on the left of picture.

A view of Amarante station on the narrow-gauge Tamega line. *Ian Peaty*

In this more recent photograph a Series 9500 railcar, bought second-hand from Yugoslavia and re-engineered with 200hp Volvo diesel engines, is seen at Amarante.

Livracao to Aramante in 1909, running along the steeply graded gorge of the Tamega River. The rest of the line was opened in stages, the final section, to Arco de Baulhe, opening in 1949, the last extension to Portugal's narrow-gauge network.

From the start the locomotives used were Henschel Mallets, which hauled freight, passenger and mixed trains until their final days in the early 1970s. As with the other narrow-gauge lines, most of the traffic was in the lower southern section between Livracao and Amarante, so from 1948 the passenger services were well catered for by three Series 9100 Swedish railcars. In 2002 these were replaced by Series 9500 (LVR2000) railcars bought second-hand from Yugoslavia and rebuilt with 200hp Volvo engines. Series 9020 diesel locomotives were also used over the whole line.

The line from Amarante to Arco de Baulhe closed in 1990 after just 40 years of service. The section south of Amarante to Livracao continued until 2009, when it was forced to close for urgent track repair work, and remains closed.

These Portuguese narrow-gauge lines, although all closed apart from the Vouga line, could offer so much to tourism if one or two of them could be brought back to life before nature claims them for all time. They run through breathtaking landscapes and quaint villages that would be a must, not only for rail enthusiasts, but also for tourists who wanted to see the real Portugal away from the big towns and motorways that are gradually invading its lovely countryside.

Spain

As a result of being one of the poorest and politically unstable countries in Western Europe at that time, the first railway was not opened until 1848. This was a short line between Barcelona and Mataro, constructed by two British engineers. The building of railways on a larger scale did not commence until the 1850s, but a decision had been made to use broad gauge track of 1674mm (5ft 5^{13}/$_{16}$ ins) for the main railway routes. This has caused problems latterly now that rail travel connects most European countries utilising the standard gauge track. However, the new high speed lines are now laid as standard gauge.

As broad gauge construction was expensive most minor routes were constructed using 1000mm (metre gauge) track, especially in the poorer areas of Spain.

The Spanish Civil War caused extensive damage to the railway network and in 1939 the unreliable broad gauge network was nationalised as RENFE (Red National de los

Located in the Castile-Leon Region, Salamanca has a very modern station rebuilt and opened in 2001. As well as local there are medium and long distance services to Madrid, Coimbra, Lisbon, San Sebastian and Santander etc. The expansive yard can be seen in the middle distance.

This RENFE Class 334-03-1 diesel-electric on shunting duties in Salamanca yard was built by Vossloh Espania/EMD in 2007 for the Iberian broad gauge. It has a top speed of 120 mph (200 km/h) and is mainly used for passenger services.

Another Iberian gauge diesel-electric Class 333-328-3 sits idling in the yard. Built in 2005 by Alstom it includes digital control and power electronics. It can attain 75mph (120km/h) and is used mainly for freight.

This is a medium distance, 3 car DMU Class 599-15, ready to depart from Salamanca for Zaragoza. It was built in 2009 at the CAF plant in the Basque region of Spain. It is capable of 100 mph (160 km/h) and mainly used for regional services.

Ferrocarriles Espania-National Network of Spanish Railways). The narrow gauge lines followed suit in the 1950s and are known as FEVE (Ferrocarriles de Via Estrecha - Narrow Gauge Railways).

It was not until the end of the Franco regime in the 1970s that any positive changes started and Spain is now modernising its railway network and beginning to catch up with the rest of Western Europe.

Note: The photos are of Salamanca station and yard. The original station was the terminus for the 83.9-mile (135km) line (closed 1985) that connected with Barca d'Alva station at the terminus of the Iberian broad gauge, Portuguese Douro line from Porto (see Portuguese section).

Ferrocarril de Soller (Palma to Soller Railway)

The Spanish sunshine holiday island of Majorca (Spanish name Mallorca) delights in a most scenic narrow-gauge railway that connects the capital, Palma, with the small and attractive town of Soller near the north-west coast. But that's not all, as there is also a secondary short tramway that connects Soller town with the Port of Soller. Both railways are of 914mm (3-foot) gauge and are powered by overhead electricity via pantograph pick-ups. Palma station is in the Place de Espania on the north-east side of town.

The engineer responsible for the construction of the railway was Pedro Garau and the contractor was Luis Bovio. Construction started from each end and the line was opened on 16 April 1912 using steam locomotives, the first being an 0-4-0 tank engine built in 1891 by Falcon Engine & Car Works Ltd of Loughborough, England, to Works No 198 and named *Maria Lussa*. Locos Nos 1 *Soller*, 2 *Palma* and 3 *Bunyola* were also delivered for the opening. The veranda teak coaches were supplied by Carde and Escoriaza.

Today freight traffic is very limited and the railway relies on tourism for its income, but is very much as it was in the beginning, apart from the 1,200V DC catenary electrification, which was installed on 14 July 1929, with four power coaches with Siemens Schuckert-Brill motors of 360hp with a tare weight of 33 tonnes. Colour-light signalling has also been installed.

Leaving Palma station, the single line runs on the level through the streets of the town before opening out into the countryside to continue its 17-mile (27.3km) climb to Soller. The line passes through 13 tunnels, the longest of which is 1.8 miles (2.9km) through the

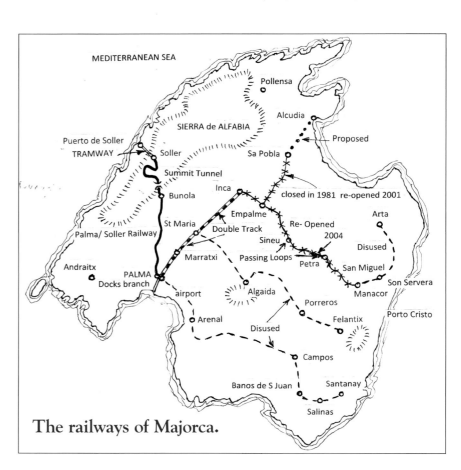

The railways of Majorca.

Locomotive No 3 arrives at Palma with its train from Soller.

At Palma terminus, electric locomotive No 2 is almost ready to leave
with a train for the 17-mile (27.3km) journey to Soller.

Sierra de Alfabia mountain range, and over several viaducts. The journey is unforgettable as the train rattles its way through the rocky terrain with wooded hillsides and olive and lemon groves – and in today's world of continuous track it is very nostalgic to hear the soporific 'rhythm of the rails' as they emit their clickety-clack.

The first major station is Son Sardina, which is an interchange with the Palma-University Line 1 Metro. The second is Bunyola, with its single low platform, passing loop and sidings at each side of the single track. Point levers use a very economic system of combined point lever coupled with an extended vertical pole surmounted by a round disc with a central hole and painted red. When the

Locomotive No 2, en route to Soller, is about to enter the longest tunnel on the line, at 1.8 miles (2.9km) under the Sierra de Alfabia range of mountains.

No 2, having arrived at Soller terminus, will now run round for its journey back to Palma.

This old truck at Soller has been converted to produce a unique catenary inspection and repair vehicle.

points are set for a clear line ahead, the disc is parallel with the track, but when switched for an adjacent line it is face-on to the driver.

Reaching the terminus at Soller, the line opens up into an attractive area with large plane trees scattered around. Here also is the workshop and stabling point for the electric locomotives, two engine sheds, one of two roads and the other of three, and a large repair shed with pits. A central turntable allows easy movement of stock into the various sheds. Also some open wagons can be seen, used for the transport of timber, and there are two small turntables for the platform wagons adjacent to the goods shed.

At Soller a small open wagon containing stores and track maintenance equipment stands next to a small turntable, with a similar one just behind.

Locomotive No 1 with a train from Soller makes its way through the streets of Palma, approaching the station.

The Soller Tramway

This additional short length of tramway was an afterthought, 4.8km long and opened in 1913 as an overhead electric system. It had to be built from the high-level terminus at Soller in order that the principal line from Palma could be eligible for a Government grant, which required an overall length of railway in excess of 30km. As the length of the 'main line' was 27.3km, the short tramway down to the coastal section of the town was sufficient to ensure that the grant was paid!

This line is a true tramway as it traverses mainly roads leading down from the joint terminus station at Soller on the hillside overlooking the coast. The trams are stabled in the same area as the railway, utilising three roads into a shed adjoining the main locomotive shed. The whole complex is gated for overnight security.

The tramway was built to the same 3-foot gauge and has always been powered by electricity. The power cars have two axles, in contrast to the bogies of the main line stock, powered by Siemens 35hp motors at 600V DC. More recently, with increased passenger volumes, five former converted Lisbon horse-drawn trams dating from the 1890s have been acquired and re-gauged to 3 feet. These smaller power cars have only one pantograph, but haul similar open-sided coaches of the 'toast-rack' type. Externally the coaches are match-boarded and in natural wood colour. All power units have large electric lamps front and rear.

On leaving Soller high-level terminus the trams run down the narrow street into the main square,

Tram No 24 creeps through Soller town square towards the port

squeezing between the many tables and chairs of the local cafes. There are passing loops, and on reaching the seashore the line runs alongside the beach wall and road leading to the port.

Terminating at the port, there is a run-round loop and the line finishes about 200 yards (180m) further along the road.

No 23 pauses at a tram stop just outside Soller's main square, where there is a passing loop.

Tram No 2 runs round at Soller's port terminus to pick up its coaches for the trip back to the town terminus at Soller.

Other railways

The increasing tourism and commercial expansion over the past 15 years has seen other railways on the island being developed and constructed, operated by TIB (Transport de les Illes Balears). As one would expect, the lines radiate from the intermodal station on Place de Espania, adjacent to the Soller line station.

The Metro has two lines. Line 1 terminates at the UIB University and Line 2 in the suburb of Marratxi, and each journey takes a maximum of 15 minutes.

There is also the main line running north-east to Sa Pobla via Inca, with a branch at Inca running south-east to Mallorca's second city, Manacor, with journey times of 56 minutes and 70 minutes respectively.

These new railways use metre-gauge track (3ft 3 in) instead of the 3-foot gauge used on the Soller Railway. In fact, the choice of the 3-foot gauge arose from British influence, who built Majorca's first railway from Palma to Inca and the central north region, opening in 1875 as the Majorca Railway Company. This was nationalised in 1951 and became FEVE in 1961. All lines were previously steam-hauled, and over the years some 67 steam locomotives have worked on this delightful island in the Mediterranean Sea.

Although Switzerland is a small, landlocked and largely mountainous country in the middle of Europe, it is well served by its various railway networks. To describe them all in detail is too large and complex a subject, so this account will be limited to 'snapshots' of Montreux, Zermatt, Davos and Klosters – but first some background on the three rail networks involved.

Swiss Federal railways

The country's main cities, towns and commuter areas (Bern, Basle, Zurich, Geneva, Montreux and Lucerne) are served by Swiss Federal Railways, the standard-gauge national railway company based in Bern. The company name is normally shown on the side of rolling stock as 'SBB-CFF-FFS', denoting its name in the three languages spoken in the country, German, French and Italian.

Swiss Federal Railways came into being as a state-owned venture in January 1902, and was the result of nationalising nine privately owned smaller companies.

Since 1999 the company has been a special stock corporation with its shares being held by the Swiss Confederation and the Swiss Cantons

Railways of Switzerland
(featured in this section)

GERMANY

Basel
Lake Constance

Olten
Zurich
Lake Zurich
AUSTRIA

Lake Neuchateel
Lucerne
Zug

FRANCE
Neuchatel
SWITZERLAND

Bern
Brianz
Fluelen
Chur
Davos

GOLDEN PASS Line
Thun
Interlaken
BERNINA EXPRESS

Lake Geneva
Lausanne
Jungfraujoch
JUNGFRAU RAILWAY
GLAZIER EXPRESS
Andermat
St Moritz

Vevey
Montreux

Brig
Poschiavo

Geneva

Zermatt
Lake Maggiore
Lugano

ITALY
Lake Como

One of the most prolific standard-gauge electric locomotives employed by Swiss Federal Railways, the Re 460 Series, entered service between 1991 and 1996. A total of 119 were built by SLM Winterthur and are powered by the overhead catenary system of 15kV/16 Hz AC.

(Regions). At that time the freight services were split off into SBB Cargo.

Today the network consists of 3,011km (1,882 miles) of standard-gauge track, which is virtually all electrified with an overhead 15kV/16 Hz AC catenary system.

There are also the narrow gauge railways.

An SBB diesel-electric locomotive built by GEC-Alstom in Spain in 1994 rests near Geneva. A total of 40 of these Bo-Bo engines were manufactured, and they have a maximum speed of 50mph (80km/h).

An SBB Cargo diesel tractor, No 127 of Type TM 232, undertakes shunting duties by the main line between Geneva and Montreux. There are a total of 32 in service, having been rebuilt for SBB Cargo; they were originally in service from 1971.

SBB Class Te 111 No 155 is an electric shunter, supporting a rather large pantograph to collect its 15kV from the overhead catenary system.

The Matterhorn Gotthard Bahn

The Matterhorn Gotthard Bahn (MGB) is a privately owned company originally known as the BZV Bahn (Brig-Visp-Zermatt Bahn). A metre-gauge (3ft 3 in) railway, it operates in the Rhone Valley and also climbs up from Brig to Zermatt in the Mattertal, which is 1,605.2 metres (5,266.6ft) above sea level. Zermatt, of course, is dominated by the Matterhorn. The distance from Brig to Zermatt is 44km and largely uses the centre rack to assist adhesion.

The BZV also forms part of the line from Zermatt to Davos and St Moritz, which is mostly single track with tight curves and steep gradients. This is a most beautiful trip and, once taken, is not forgotten. The most impressive way to maximise the view and enjoyment is to take the 'Glacier Express'.

In January 2003 BZV merged with the Furka-Oberalp Bahn (FO) to become Matterhorn-Gotthard Bahn. The network is electrified with an overhead catenary system working at 11kV/16⅔Hz AC.

The Rhatische Bahn

The Rhatische Bahn (RhB) is another privately owned metre-gauge railway that operates in the eastern part of the country in the canton of Graubuden. It is the largest of the privately owned companies and serves the major tourist resorts of Davos and St Moritz. The lines interchange with Swiss Federal Railways at Chur and Landquart. RhB locomotives take over from the Matterhorn-Gotthard locomotives at the canton border station of Disentis. The 'Glacier Express' also stops here for the locomotive change.

The Rhatische Bahn has 384km (240 miles) of metre-gauge (3ft 3⅜in) track with 11kV/16⅔Hz AC overhead catenary electrification. The 62km (38.75 miles) of the Bernina line uses 1,000V DC fed by an overhead catenary system.

Montreaux

Montreux is a cultural city surrounded by hillsides covered in vineyards and gardens with an attractive lakeside promenade. It is well served by local transport, including a trolleybus service between Montreux and Vevey.

Montreux station was opened in 1861 and is located on a hillside in the middle of the town, overlooking Lake Geneva. It is somewhat of a rarity, as it accommodates three different gauges across seven tracks, although due to earlier engineering works track two has been removed.

The SBB uses Platforms 1 and 3, which are

A standard-gauge Class RaBe 523, forming an SBB electric 'FLIRT' train (Fast, Light, Regional Train), stands at Montreux's Platform 1. It is a four-car set that can be walked through with eight automatic doors. They were built from 2004 by Stadler.

Just arrived at Montreux from Les Avants is an MOB Golden Pass metre-gauge train hauled by Class GDe 4/4 electric locomotive No 6004 *Interlaken*. This line uses an 850V DC overhead catenary system.

the only through tracks and are standard gauge. There are frequent SBB regional trains that stop here, mainly of the FLIRT variety (Fast, Light Regional Trains).

The other two gauges are metre gauge (1,000mm/3ft 3 in), used by the Golden Pass lines, and 800mm (2ft 7½in), used by the Rochers-de-Naye line, both of which terminate at Montreux.

Golden Pass is a services company that manages and operates train services for Compagnie du Chemin de fer Montreux Oberland Bernois (MOB) and Transports Montreux-Vevey Riviera (MVR).

MOB (Compagnie du Chemin de fer Montreux Oberland Bernois)

MOB trains normally depart from Montreux's Platform 5, with arrivals at Platform 6. The line uses metre-gauge track with electrical power from an 850V DC overhead catenary system.

The route winds its way through beautiful countryside, woods and vineyards above Lake Geneva and onwards to Gstaad and Zweisimmen, where there is also a branch to Lenk. Zweisimmen also offers interchange with the standard-gauge track of the Bern-Lotschberg-Simplon Railway to Spiez and onward travel to Interlaken and Lucerne. The MOB does not utilise any rack system, which means that the maximum incline is no more than 7.3%.

Some services use the 'Panoramic' coaching stock, with observation cars at each end and the locomotive in the middle in 'push-pull' mode.

The local trains on this MOB route terminate at Fontanivent, Sonzier and Les Avents.

This is an MOB Golden Pass 'Panoramic' observation, operated in a 'push-pull' combination with the electric locomotive situated in the middle of the train: It is just about ready to leave Montreux for Les Avents.

MVR (Transport Montreux-Vevey-Riviera)

The third rail gauge at Montreux station is that of the Montreux-Glion-Rochers-de-Naye railway, 800mm (2ft 7½in). Its electrification is by overhead catenary at 850V DC, and track adhesion is maintained by the use of the rack-and-pinion method based on the Carl Roman Abt design.

Services for this line use Platforms 7 and 8. The line is 7.6km (4¾ miles) long and runs through a series of tunnels, changing direction on several occasions and providing views of Lake Geneva from both sides of the train. When it reaches Rochers-de-Naye the views of the lake and the Alps are spectacular. At the highest point the line is at an elevation of 1,973 metres (6,473 feet). This is also the home of 'Marmot Paradise', where several varieties of these creatures are kept in their natural habitat.

The railway owns several styles of railcar dating from 1939 to 2010.

Top right: Modern and stylish Montreux-Vevey-Riviera (MVR) Class Be 2/6 No 7004, a two-car electric set, is about to leave Montreux for a local service to Fontanivent.

Right: This MOB two-car set, Class ABDe 8/8 No 4004 *Fribourg*, is from an older generation, built in 1968 by the SIG/BBC/SAAS consortium.

Top left: MVR Class Bhe 2/4 No 204, built in 1939 by SLM/ BBC, is a fine example of a Montreux-Rochers-de-Naye electric single railcar. Note the Abt rack between the 2ft 7½in (800mm) track. The MVR uses 850V DC via an overhead catenary system.

Above: This small, odd-looking electric shunter was located at the MVR yard and workshop in Vevey, a short distance from Montreux. It was apparently put together from a variety of parts from retired Lucerne trams!

Left: An MVR railcar emerges from the tunnel into Platform 8 at Montreux. This is one of the latest railcars built by MOB Cherex/Siemens in 2010 and displaying the Golden Pass livery. Note the other railcar in the siding, No 303 *Villeneuve*, built by SLM/Siemens in 1983.

Zermatt

The Zermatt electric railway provides spectacular mountain views, one of many such narrow-gauge railways in Switzerland. *Ian Peaty*

Zermatt is 1,605.2m (5,267 feet) above sea level in the Mattertal, Valais region, and its obvious attraction is winter sports, but it is equally attractive in the summer months. The town is at the foot of the mountains, the biggest and most infamous being the Matterhorn.

Zermatt station is situated at the end on the main street. An avalanche destroyed it in 1966, but it was rebuilt and concrete avalanche proofing was completed over the top by 1989.

Road vehicles are not allowed into Zermatt unless by permission or emergency. Vehicular traffic in the town consists of small battery-powered carts adapted as vans and taxis, and hotel guest and luggage pick-ups. No tourist traffic can go any further up the valley road than the town of Tasch, where visitors have to take the shuttle train up to Zermatt.

There is plenty of rail activity at Zermatt with the frequent arrivals and departures of the Tasch shuttle trains, trains to and from Brig and Visp, and of course the 'Glacier Express'.

A 'Crocodile' Class Ge 6/6 approaches Zermatt from Brig. *Ian Peaty*

Gornergratbahn (GGB)

Opposite Zermatt station is the Gornergratbahn (GGB), part of the group that also owns MGB. It is a 9.35km (5.8-mile) line that runs from its own station in Zermatt to its summit at Gornergrat, at an elevation of 3,089m (10,135 feet). The whole line uses the Abt rack system.

This metre-gauge (3ft 3 in) railway was opened in 1898 and has always been electrified. Its electrification is, however, unusual and may be unique, as it is powered by two overhead lines on a catenary system operating at 725V AC at 50Hz from a three-phase supply. The power to the unit uses two pantgraphs in parallel; they are flexibly joined but insulated from each other.

There are several stations and halts on the way to the summit, and 3.79km (2.4 miles) is double track. The views from the summit are breathtaking, especially of the Matterhorn on a clear day.

At the MGB Zermatt station there is a chord from the sidings that crosses the main street and swings in to the small siding area at the Gornergratbahn station. This enables all track and unit maintence supplies to be easily brought up from Visp and transferred directly to the Gornergratbahn.

The railway runs some older Bhe railcars built by SLM Winterthur, which entered service in 1993, and some newer Bhe railcars built by Stadler, which came into service in 2006. These have low-elevation floors and larger picture windows.

Right: Gornergratbahn Class Bhe 4/8A twin-unit railcar No 3042, in service since 1965, stands at the line's Zermatt station. Note the parallel pantographs for the three-phase 725V AC supply and the short metre-gauge chord in the foreground that connects to the main Zermatt station yard.

Below: This spectacular view with the Matterhorn in the background is the Gornergrat terminus. Just arrived are two two-unit railcars, Class Bhe 4/6 Nos 3083 and 3084, built in 2006 by Stadler.

'Glacier Express'

Two trains depart from the MGB (Matterhorn-Gotthard Bahn) station each day, the first for Davos and the second for St Moritz. The journey time is 7hr 56min. The locomotive is normally an MGB HGe4/4 Series 3 and the train has six coaches, including a vintage restaurant car in the middle. Incidentally, the 'Glacier Express' is known as the slowest express in existence!

The route is roughly west to east through Visp, Brig, Andermatt, Disentis, Chur and Davos, or Chur to St Moritz. Arriving at Disentis the first 'Glacier Express' stops

The 'Glacier Express' climbs high above Andermatt station and the MGB yard and works. Note the start of the Abt rack between the bottom of the picture and the road.

Matterhorn Gotthard Bahn (MGB) Class Gm 3/3 diesel shunter No 72 is busy organising the 'Glacier Express' coaching arrangements for the day prior to departure from Zermatt for Davos or St Moritz.

for 43 minutes. This is the territorial limit of the MGB and from Disentis to Davos/ St Moritz it is Rhatische Bahn territory; consequently an RhB locomotive is coupled to the stock. The second 'Glacier Express' then pulls in behind the first, the MGB locomotive is uncoupled, and the coaches coupled to the last coach of the first train. The combined train then leaves Disentis en route for Chur. The line runs

along 15km (9.4 miles) of the beautiful Rhine Gorge and eventually into Chur station.

Chur is one of the interchange stations with the SBB, and for the 'Glacier Express' it is a convenient point to uncouple the two sets of coaches, couple up individual locomotives again and depart from Chur the same way that they came in, one train to Davos and the other to St Moritz.

The Davos, Klosters and Landquart line

Trains from Davos go northbound to Klosters and Landquart and southbound to Filisur. Landquart is 50km (31¼ miles) from Davos Platz, and is an interchange with SBB and the limit of Rhatische Bahn operations.

The line from Davos makes tight twists and turns, descends sharply into a tunnel then over the Landquart River bridge into Klosters station. Klosters is a busy tourist station, especially in the winter skiing period with trains arriving and departing at frequent intervals.

Maintenance vehicles are kept at Klosters for emergency situations in the vicinity, for example a diesel vehicle of Class Tm 2/2 with a crane for permanent way construction work, and a small diesel shunter of Class Tm 2/3 for departmental services and rescue situations.

Switzerland has a wealth of railway interest whether you are a a rail enthusiast or just riding the trains on holiday.

Left: At Disentis the 'Glacier Express' stops for a while as this is the boundary of the MGB operation, and a Rhatische Bahn (RhB) locomotive takes over. This is Class Ge 4/4 Series 3 No 646 *Sta Maria Val Mustair*, built in 1994 by SLM/ABB, Adtranz. It carries an advertisement for 'BUGA', an RhB season ticket.

Below: The RhB line from Davos to Klosters winds through some spectacular scenery before descending into the valley to Klosters station.

Seen at Klosters station, RhB Class Ge 4/4 Series 2 No 617 *Ilanz*, built in 1973, carries Rhatia Energie Power livery. This eastbound train is ready to leave for Scuol-Tarasp station, where it will terminate.

Classification of locomotives, multiple units, motor coaches and railcars

This subject is a complex one as the Swiss classification system has changed over the years, with the result that there is a mixture of systems in operation, but mainly defined between standard- and narrow-gauge motive power. The listings shown are condensed to describe the stock in this chapter.

Locomotives
G = Narrow-gauge locomotive used for adhesion
H = Locomotive with rack rail operation
R = Standard-gauge locomotive with higher cornering speeds (at least 110km/h – Rapid)
T = Tractor (shunter)

Multiple units, motor coaches and railcars
A = Vehicle with 1st Class
B = Vehicle with 2nd Class
C = Vehicle with 3rd Class
D = Vehicle with luggage compartment
R = Multiple unit, motor coach or railcar with higher cornering speeds (at least 110km/h – Rapid)

Traction type
e = Electric
h = Rail rack drive
m = Fuel used (diesel)

Axles
First number is drive axles
Second number is total axles
A couple of examples:

HGe 4/4 – A locomotive with rack rail operation, narrow gauge, and able to operate in adhesion mode. Its motive power is electric and it has four axles, all of which are driving axles.

RABe – A narrow-gauge multiple unit capable of higher speeds, with 1st and 2nd Class and powered by electricity.

Bhe – A multiple unit with just 2nd Class, rail rack drive only, and powered by electricity.

Be 2/6 – A multiple unit with 2nd Class only, powered by electricity and with six axles of which two are driving axles.

Manufacturers' names
SLM = Swiss Locomotive & Machine Works (Winterthur)
BBC = Brown Boverie & Cie
ABB = Asea Brown Boverie
SIG = Schweizerische Industrie Gesellschaft
SAAS = Société Anonyme des Ateliers de Secheron, Geneva
SWP = Schindler Wagon Pratteln

In the heart of the Tyrol region the standard-gauge main line from Innsbruck heads east, with a station at Jenbach. From here two narrow-gauge railways go their separate ways. The Zillertalbahn heads off up the valley to Mayrhofen, while in the opposite direction the Achenseebahn heads straight up into the mountains to terminate at the Achensee Lake.

In the terminus station at Vienna are two variations of the national railway livery. On the left is a Class 1014 Bo-Bo built in 1993, and on the right a mixed-traffic Class 2143 built from 1965.

The Zillertalbahn

From the joint triple station of Jenbach, the Zillertalbahn runs along the lovely Ziller valley to Mayrhofen, a truly delightful and typical Tyrolean village surrounded by meadows and superbly forested mountains. This private railway has a gauge of 2ft 6in (760mm) and uses conventional track, but there convention finishes as this narrow-gauge railway has the most interesting system of using 'transporter' wagons to carry OBB (Austrian State Railways) standard-gauge covered vans and tank wagons 'piggy-back'-fashion.

The line commenced construction on 26 December 1899 and was opened for business on 31 July 1902. As with most feeder branch lines, agricultural produce was the main freight, but with the Zillertalbahn it had a heavier product to convey from the magnesium mine that traded from 1929 to 1976. Today passenger trains run in the summer season every half-

This is the Zillertalbahn terminus at Mayrhofen, with 0-6-2T locomotive No 2 *Zillertal* outside the engine shed ready for the day's work.

hour. Sets of both modern and original coaches are used, with around 12 items of straight-sided, four-wheeled older stock and a diesel railcar. Locomotives Nos 1 and 2, built by Krauss Linz in 1900, were the original motive power, with No 2 *Zillertal*, Works No 4506, still in service. Two years later, fleet No 3, an 0-6-2 tank, Works No 4790, was delivered. No 5 *Garlos* is a similar tank engine built by Krauss Linz, this time in 1930. All have 'balloon' spark-

A Zillertalbahn 0-6-2T and its train leave Mayrhofen for Jenbach, where it will connect with the OBB standard-gauge and metre-gauge Achenseebahn railways – three gauges meeting in a single location!

Top: Also seen at Mayrhofen station is 0-4-0T No 6, built by Krauss in 1916, with a small spark-arrester chimney of unusual style.

Above: In Mayrhofen freight yard are two transporter wagons for carrying standard-gauge wagons, which are collected at Jenbach on the OBB main line.

arrester chimneys, but the newer locos have a much more refined, slimmer style. Three of this railway's open veranda coaches have been recently donated to the Welshpool & Llanfair Light Railway and now run on that lovely preserved narrow-gauge railway in Wales.

In the early mornings it is not unusual to hear a harmonious clanging as the surrounding hills come alive with the sound of cow bells. Lederhosen-clad young men take their herds of cows up to the mountain pastures through the town, each cow with its own bell and floral garlands around its horns – not even the raising of steam at the terminus can compete with this delightful scene.

The Archenseebahn

Because of the need to climb into the mountains, the narrow-gauge Achensee Railway uses the rack-and-pinion system initially to take the train up to a mountain plateau, where the normal two rails return for the remainder of the journey.

In 1888, Kaiser Franz Josef gave consent for the 6.78kW metre-gauge (1,000mm/3ft 3⅜in) railway to be built on the Riggenbach rack system. The journey of 45 minutes takes passengers through Alpine scenery on the 16% graded track, then levels out to pass through

The Achenseebahn is the oldest metre-gauge cog railway, built in 1889. It is 4.2 miles (6.76km) long and has three 0-4-0T steam locomotives built at Floridsdorf for the opening of the railway. *Ian Peaty*

Achenseebahn locomotive No 2 was built for the line in 1889 by Weiner Locomotivfabrik, and uses the Riggenbach rack system to negotiate the steep gradients.

lush meadows grazed by the happy cows with their melodious bells. Up here can be found the brilliant blue gentian and the white edelweiss mountain flowers.

As with the Zillertalbahn, agricultural produce was the main cargo until it ceased to be carried in 1973. Around that time the majority shares in the railway company were acquired by the Tyrolean Water Company, which was most generous in giving them to the authorities in the three villages on the line.

Six delightful four-wheeled red and cream coaches were built in 1889, four open and two enclosed, with additional closed coaches built

in 1903 and 1907 at Esslingen. For the former freight trains there were four low-sided open wagons and one high-sided, with only one covered van. Today trains normally run with two coaches with the locomotive pushing in the uphill direction. The locos, liveried in dark green with scarlet red frames and polished connecting rods, are No 1 *Theodor*, No 2 *Herman*, No 3 *Georg* and No 4 *Coal*; they were all built in 1889 by Wiener Lokomotivfabrik of Floridsdorf with Works Nos 701-704 respectively.

On 16 May 2008 a fire at the engine shed at Jenbach destroyed the building and loco No 1.

The Harz Mountain railway network

The Harz Mountains are located towards the northern part of Germany, with the highest peak, Brocken, rising to a height of 3,743 feet (1,141m). The name 'Harz' means 'mountain forest' and it certainly lives up to its name, although it is a small range surrounded by flat plains.

Until the fall of communism the area found itself in East Germany, with the metre-gauge (3ft 3 in) network preserved in a time warp. It was then owned by Deutsche Reichsbahn.

During 1993, after German unification, the railway was taken over in its entirety by the private company Harzer Schmalspurbahnen GmbH (HSB). Its shareholders are the districts of Harz and Nordhausen, the town of Quedlinburg, and other communes served by the network. The total length of the network is 140.4km (87 miles), and all routes interact. It is split into three main routes:

1: The Trans-Harz Railway, which runs south from Wernigerode to Nordhausen. In December 1898 the Nordhausen-Wernigerode Eisenbahn (NWE) company was registered and began full operations from Wernigerode via Drei Annen to Nordhausen on 27 March 1899.

2: The Brocken Railway, which branches off the Trans-Harz just after Drei Annen Hohne station to the summit of the Brocken, was fully opened in 1898 by the NWE. This is the main tourist line of the network.

3: The Selketalbahn (Selke Valley Railway), which branches off the Trans-Harz at Eisfelder Talmuhle and runs to Quedlinburg with minor branches to Hasselfelde and Harzgerode. The first section was opened in 1887 by a company registered as Gernrode-Harzgeroder Eisenbahn Gesellschaft (GHE), and ran between Gernrode and Magdesprung, later extended to include branches to Harzgerode, Hasselfelde and Eisfelder Talmuhle. It became known as the Selke Valley Railway (Selketalbahn) as it runs in the valley alongside the Selke River.

On 1 April 1949 both the NWE and GHE were placed under control of the East German Deutsche Reichsbahn until 1993.

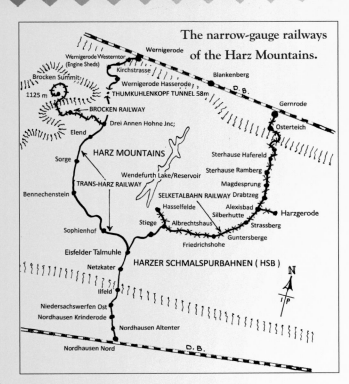

The narrow-gauge railways of the Harz Mountains.

Wernigerode Westerntor (Engine Sheds)
Wernigerode
Kirchstrasse
Blankenberg
Brocken Summit
1125 m
Wernigerode Hasserode
THUMKUHLENKOPF TUNNEL 58m
D. B.
Gernrode
BROCKEN RAILWAY
Osterteich
Drei Annen Hohne Jnc;
Elend
HARZ MOUNTAINS
Sterhause Hafereld
Sorge
Sterhause Ramberg
Wendefurth Lake/Reservoir
Magdesprung
TRANS-HARZ RAILWAY
SELKETALBAHN RAILWAY
Drabtzeg
Bennechenstein
Hasselfelde
Alexisbad
Silberhutte
Harzgerode
Stiege
Albrechtshaus
Strassberg
Sophienhof
Guntersberge
Friedrichshohe
Eisfelder Talmuhle
HARZER SCHMALSPURBAHNEN (HSB)
Netzkater
N
Ilfeld
Niedersachswerfen Ost
Nordhausen Krinderode
Nordhausen Altenter
Nordhausen Nord
D. B.

The Brocken Railway

The terminus for the Brocken is on the outskirts of the delightful medieval town of Wernigerode, located in the foothills of the Harz Mountains and overlooked by its castle. It has many carved and painted wooden houses in the old town centre, with an outer modern suburban development that includes a chocolate factory and a cake factory, with a medium-sized brewery that produces, among others, an excellent 'Dunkel' brown beer – what a lovely mixture!

The station of HSB, the owning company, is just a short walk from the town centre and is located immediately adjacent to the DB standard-gauge line with connections to Hannover, Goslar, Leipzig and Berlin. The HSB runs around six direct steam-hauled trains to Brocken and back every day during the summer season, and a little fewer during the winter.

In the HSB yard is the engine shed and turntable and the water and coaling point. Early morning is the time for intense activity as several of the large and impressive 2-10-2 tank locomotives are steamed up ready for the day's work, resplendent in their black livery with scarlet front and rear buffer beams and wheels.

The passenger coaches waiting at the platform are livered in red and cream with the luggage/brake van in all-over deep red. They all have veranda access at each end.

The journey time to Brocken is 1hr

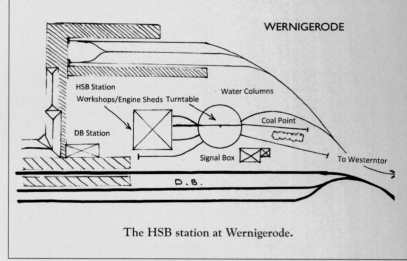

The HSB station at Wernigerode.

Former East German Harz Railway (ESB) Mallet 0-4-0+0-4-0T No 995906-5, with a veranda luggage van at Wernigerode. *Ian Peaty*

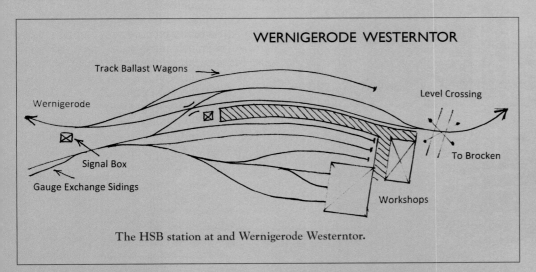

WERNIGERODE WESTERNTOR

Track Ballast Wagons

Wernigerode

Level Crossing

Signal Box

To Brocken

Gauge Exchange Sidings

Workshops

The HSB station at and Wernigerode Westerntor.

40min. Four minutes after leaving the Wernigerode terminus the first of the six intermediate stations is reached at Wernigerode Westerntor. Here are the coach sidings and workshops, while three diesel locomotives are stored here for assembling the coaches for each train and taking them to the terminus. These locos are notable for their bulkiness, having been converted from standard gauge. Two sidings lead off to make connection with the DB line, and are used as gauge transfer sidings where standard-gauge wagons 'piggy-backing' on the narrow-gauge wagons can usually be seen. These transfer sidings are especially useful to the track maintenance team, as four-

Above: Two immaculately turned-out 2-10-2Ts, Nos 7247 and 236 stand in Wernigerode yard coaled and watered ready for the day's work on the Harz Brocken network. They generate up to 700hp and were built between 1954 and 1956.

Left: Another view of No 236 all ready for the day's work, and what a fine example of care and attention over the years with its resplendent black body and red wheels!

wheeled aggregate hopper wagons are 'piggy-backed' on their own dedicated narrow-gauge bogie wagons and coupled to each other by a long steel connecting rod. These wagons are stored in their own designated loop siding opposite the passenger platform. Freight traffic is no longer operated, although there are a few wagons at various locations.

After leaving Wernigerode Westerntor, the single track runs alongside an attractive residential road and stream, then curves right over a major road junction on the outskirts of the town. The train then starts climbing steadily through the foothills with deciduous trees beginning to close in on both sides. After approximately 20 minutes the train passes through the 58-metre-long Thumkuhlenkopf Tunnel, the only one on the Harz network. The 2-10-2 locomotive is then beginning to work harder, making all those glorious sounds associated with steam-hauled trains.

The next major stop is at Drei Annen Hohne station, 50 minutes from Wernigerode. Strictly speaking, the Brocken line starts here, as the line from Wernigerode is part of the Trans-Harz Railway to Nordhausen. It is a welcome attractive open space after 33 minutes of fairly dense forest. The station has a side platform with the station office and two island platforms, all of which are in use.

A local road serves the station, and a hotel providing a good lunch sits up on a bank with views over the railway.

After a 13-minute stop for the locomotive to take on water, the train leaves for its onward journey. A short distance out of the station the lines split, with the Trans-Harz route turning sharply to the left towards Nordhausen, while the Brocken train heads up the much steeper climb towards the summit. The climb becomes steeper and the curves tighter as the track follows the rocky contours, something that only narrow-gauge railways can do. Views are restricted to pine tree trunks and boulders.

After 51 minutes the view opens up as the train nears the summit. There is not much of railway interest here, just the halt and a run-round loop ready for the return journey. There is a scattering of old, grey concrete buildings from the Cold War, which once housed both Russian and East German troops who operated and guarded the Soviet listening equipment that scanned across the border into West Germany. The railway continued to run during this time to transport troops and equipment,

Right: A standard-gauge four-wheeled hopper wagon is 'piggy-backing' on a metre-gauge bogie wagon used for deployment of track maintenance aggregate around the Harz network.

Above: No 7241 is being turned in Wernigerode yard and directed onto the correct track ready for departure.

and a barrier fence was erected around the military zone to keep out unwanted visitors. These buildings have now been converted into more hospitable places for tourists including a large refectory area for food and drink and a shop. After the Cold War the track was relaid, and in 1992 the line was reopened to the public once more.

The views from the top are breathtaking, but statistically the mountain is covered in fog and rain for 300 days of the year, so choose your moment!

Above: The 2-10-2 is pulling hard up the steady incline to the summit of the Brocken. Most of the journey is through dense forest and rocky terrain.

Left: Stopped at the signal, the train waits for the line ahead to clear. A track maintenance gang take a break from their morning's work.

At Drei Annen the locos take on water and generate interest from the tourists. The train on the left will continue up to the Brocken summit while the one on the right will divert left towards Nordhausen.

The Selketal Railway (Selke Valley Railway)

This line has the least traffic on the network, although some goods traffic is still active. Most of the passenger services are for local people and are catered for by HSB railbuses with just a couple of steam services each day.

The junction station of Alexisbad in the densely wooded Selke Valley is approximately halfway along its total route length. This unmanned station is worth a mention, built with stone up to the first floor and wood above, with an attached timber-framed goods shed, all looking in need of some care and attention. The journey from here to Gernrode and Quedlinburg is along the picturesque Selke Valley.

This line is not short of quaint rolling stock. Its railcars of varying ages, shapes and sizes are mainly used by the

Above: This unique little diesel railcar was built for the Gernrode-Harzgerode Railway in 1933 and became a workmen's tool wagon after the Second World War. It was numbered 187.001 by the East German Deutsche Reichsbahn. It has now been restored and can carry 34 passengers. It is seen here at Alexisbad station on the Selketalbahn.

Left: Beautifully turned-out 2-6-2T No 6001 has just arrived at Gernrode station, where the train will terminate.

locals for their shopping expeditions on the short branch line to Harzgerode.

The trip along this stretch of line is through the winding Selke Valley with lush trees and rocky cuttings beside the narrow river. The train crosses several minor roads on the level and passes stations that are no longer in use except as request stops. One proudly advertises a local beer, but sadly the bar is no longer open. Depending on what train is boarded from Alexisbad, it might be hauled by a 2-10-2T or a 2-6-2T.

At Gernrode the station has a yard and an engine shed, several sidings, and coaling and water facilities. On the far side a few wagons and a small snowplough can be seen among the grass and trees.

Gernrode was also the former terminus of a standard-gauge branch line owned by Deutsche Reichsbahn (DR) of the German Democratic Republic. It now stands aloof, its previous grandeur gradually showing signs of serious dereliction.

Leaving Gernrode, the narrow-gauge track is then diverted onto the bed of the previous standard-gauge track. This engineering work was completed in 2006. The line is now reasonably straight and flat as it makes its way to Quedlinburg, and there are still a couple of sections where the old standard-gauge track can be seen.

Nearing Quedlinburg the DB line sweeps in from the left and the two lines run parallel into the station, which has regular services between Halberstadt, Magdeburg, Berlin and Leipzig. The HSB train terminates here and the locomotive runs round in readiness for its return journey along the Selke Valley line.

It is a short walk from Quedlinburg station into the middle of the medieval town with its attractive square, and it has deservedly been declared a UNESCO Heritage Town.

Harz Railway network rolling stock

At the time of writing the network has 25 steam locomotives, of which around 15 are operational. They consist of 18 2-10-2Ts (mostly 1950s vintage), two 0-6-0Ts, a 2-6-2T and four 0-4-4-0T Mallets built between 1897 and 1956.

The network also has 13 diesel railcars of varying types, of which 11 are operational, together with 12 diesel locomotives, of which only five appear to be operational. The three diesel shunters, Nos 199 010-012, have all been converted from standard to metre gauge and were built between 1964 and 1990. It is believed that only one is operational. They are designated for shunting duties in and around Wernigerode Westerntor, and diesels Nos 199 861 to 892 have also been converted from standard to metre gauge and used to haul work trains, breakdown and goods trains together with shunting and snow clearance duties. They were built around 1976 and are stabled at Wernigerode and Nordhausen.

A relatively new diesel railcar, No 187-015 was built by DBAG-Wittenberge as a prototype for the HSB. It came into service in June 1996 and resides at Nordhausen depot.

Left: Men in action! 2-6-2T No 6001 is having its firebox emptied and the sand dome filled with sand after finishing its work for the day at Gernrode.

Left: This rather oversize diesel-hydraulic DR Class V100 was originally a standard-gauge locomotive and was one of ten converted to metre gauge from 1966 for the Harz network, where they are known as 'Harz camels'. They were converted as replacements for steam, which of course didn't happen, so several have now been sold to be converted back to standard gauge. Those left are used for marshalling carriages and snow clearance.

The Rhine is the longest river in Germany, flowing north from its origins in Switzerland through Germany and Holland and discharging into the North Sea near Rotterdam. It is the 'river motorway' for local and continental barge traffic, with numerous river and canal connections to many areas of northern Europe.

In the Middle Rhine area, and especially along the picturesque and steep-sided Rhine Gorge, there are double rail tracks on both banks running only a few metres from the river, along which both freight and passenger trains run every few minutes in both directions. The freight trains far outnumber the passenger trains, as major cities, industries and inland ports are concentrated further downstream, cities such as Cologne, Dusseldorf and Duisburg, the largest inland port in Europe, where much of the rail freight traffic originates. The Ruhr also joins the Rhine at this point, but most of the heavy industry along this river has now been replaced by lighter and more technical industries. A variety of electric and diesel locomotives can be seen along these tracks operated by Deutsche Bundesbahn (DB) and its European railway partners.

Cologne (Koln) is the major railway hub with connections to the Ruhr and manufacturing towns such as Dusseldorf and Dortmund, with Aachen to the west making connections with Belgium, Holland and soon with high-speed trains to the UK.

Cologne's first station was built in 1843 with a line to Antwerp; the station was rebuilt during the early 1900s and again after the last war due to Allied bombing. The metal bow-arched bridges over the Rhine were also put out of use, and these too have been rebuilt to a similar design. The station today has 11 platforms with a massive single arched roof spanning them, with five smaller arches extending towards the river. Overlooking this intensive scene is the twin-spired cathedral. The bridges today have six tracks laid on three bow-string arches spanning 409 metres. The station handles 1,230 trains daily, almost all of which are operated by the state carrier, Deutsche Bundesbahn. They consist of local S-Bahn and Regional Bahn trains, Regional Expresses and Inter City Expresses, known as ICE trains.

Upstream, at the southern end of the Rhine Gorge, is Mannheim on the east bank, with the industrialised town of Ludwigshafen almost opposite on the west bank. The two towns are connected by road and rail bridges.

Ludwigshafen has some industrial sites that occupy the riverside including chemical manufacturing and grain storage facilities, with plants having their own rail sidings and a variety of industrial locomotives.

Again, the main lines follow the river, with freight trains often consisting of a mix of wagons transporting the products of the various manufacturers. The greater distances on the continent make the continued use of these

The 'Rheingold Express' on private charter carries a special livery, and is seen here hauled by Class V170 Co-Co diesel No MY1142, built in 1955 and owned by Braunschweiger Bahn Service (Brunswick Railway Service – bsbs). It is passing over the level crossing at Assmannshausen.

mixed trains necessary, and they are sometimes double-headed.

In contrast to the modern DB image was the use of fireless locomotives seen in 2005. Two types were working in the Ludwigshafen area at one location. This type of locomotive was designed in Germany in the 1880s and makes use of a readily available supply of steam from a stationary boiler at the works; they are most economical as they only use the stored steam when actually working. Manufacturers include Hanomag, Borsig & Henschel, Arnold Jung and Hohenzollern. These fireless locos were manufactured into the 1990s, so the contrast is all the more pronounced when seen alongside the splendour of the streamlined white ICE trains and the resplendent diesel and electric locomotives and coaches in their scarlet livery.

Left: Cologne station and the city's cathedral overlook the Rhine Bridge, which carries seven rail tracks. On the right is a Class 038 4-6-0 of the old Prussian Railways, while a Class 01 'Pacific' is about to cross over the river. *Ian Peaty*

Below: An Inter-City Express (ICE) streamlined train approaches the station across the famous Rhine Bridge, which was heavily bombed during the war and subsequently rebuilt.

Leaving Cologne station is a DB Class 146 high-speed passenger locomotive built in 2001, with double-deck coaches.

Above: Travelling through the Rhine Gorge is a Class 101 Co-Co electric locomotive built in the late 1990s hauling double-deck coaches in DB scarlet livery.

Right: At Mannheim the coal-fired power station uses its own fireless boiler shunting locomotive, a Class TYR-C Type 5 0-6-0 built by Dampfspeicher Locomotive Bauart of Meningen. This is one of several locations that utilises its own railway.

Italy

Italy consists of its mainland and the two important islands of Sicily at its southernmost tip and Sardinia, basking in the Mediterranean Sea about 125 miles to the west. The mainland is a country of contrasts. It is approximately 750 miles (1,200km) from north to south and averages 100 miles (160km) from east to west. The north is the most industrialised, where the population is greatest, the way of life and food are influenced by the north of Europe, and winters are colder. The rail network reflects the need to connect the important centres, including Milan, Bologna, Verona, Venice and of course the Italian Lakes. Main lines also connect Italy with France and Switzerland through the Simplon and Gotthard tunnels, with other connections to Austria and Slovenia.

Further south everything starts to become more Mediterranean, with more sun, vineyards, olive groves, higher temperatures and a people generally more relaxed and friendly. The larger centres, such as Rome, Naples and Florence, are further apart, and the rail network becomes more spread out the further south it goes.

The railways were nationalised in 1905 as Ferrovie dello Stato (FS), with its operating company Trenitalia. There were also a few private lines, some still in existence, especially in the southerly regions.

Apart from the odd narrow-gauge line, the FS and private lines are the standard gauge of 4ft 8½in (1,435mm), some non-electrified and others

Turin's Porta Nuova station opened in 1864; there is a plaque dedicated to the two Stephensons on the facade. This is Italy's third busiest terminus station, and now has 20 platforms. *Ian Peaty*

electrified, employing catenary systems supplying 3,000V DC, 25kV AC, 50Hz, 15kV AC and 750V DC. There is a large variety of rolling stock across the nationalised sector and the private operators, including electric and diesel locomotives, electric and diesel multiple units, and diesel railcars and trailers.

Apart from local, regional and inter-city trains, there are high-speed Trenitalia 'Frecciarossa' ('Red Arrow') and 'Italo' trains running regularly up and down the country, as well as connecting with their northerly neighbours.

Once away from the main-line network the lines travelling through rural areas can be very overgrown with grass, the stations run-down and the rolling stock in need of replacement. However, where stations are manned the staff are only too pleased to have a chat, which adds to the attraction and charm of these country railways.

Right: A Trenitalia 'Eurostar' Class ETR500 leaves Venice Santa Lucia station for Rome. The station is situated on Venice island by the Grand Canal and crosses a causeway to the Italian mainland.

Below left: Trenord Class ETR425 No 065 leaves Strese station by Lake Maggiore. Built by Alstom in 2014, these units operate on a 3,000V DC catenary system.

Below right: Trenitalia Cargo Class E655 No 419 is one of a class built between 1975 and 1989. Originally for mixed traffic, they were converted for freight operation with lower gearbox ratios. These also operate on 3,000V DC.

Top right: An NTV 'Italo' electric set stands at Florence's Santa Maria Novello station ready to leave for Milan.

Centre right: Class D445 No 068 is also seen at Santa Maria Novello station, Florence.

Below right: The Trenitalia ETR 610 Class are seven-coach EMUs, built in 2009 and used on Italian/Swiss services. They operate on three power modes to accommodate the two countries' different catenary power systems.

Above: Trenord Class 464 No 198 calls at Varenna station, above Lake Como, heading for Milan. The driver of the driver-only train shows how the job is done!

Far left: A fine example of a Class 464 locomotive, No. 639 at Ostuni station on the main line in Puglia between Bari and Brindisi. They are the work horse of Trenitalia and around 700 are in operation. Built by Bombardier from 1999 onwards, they can operate in a push-pull mode with control at the other end of the train.

Left: Ceglie Messapica has a very rural aspect with an FSE AD44 unit just arrived from Lecce en route to Francavilla Fontana. This diesel railbus was built in 1978 by Fiat and looked and sounded its age.

Far left: Giovanni was a very helpful and pleasant Station Master at the Ferrovie Sud-Est (FSE) country station of Ceglie Messapica in the Puglia Region. He spoke proudly about being an employee of FSE.

Left: This is a new (by comparison) DMU type, ATR 22 No 016. A total of 27 were built for FSE by Pesa of Poland between 2008 and 2010. This set is at Gallipoli (Puglia), awaiting a return trip to Lecce.

Sardinia

The large Italian island of Sardinia is just 7.7 miles (12.25km) from the southern tip of Corsica in the Mediterranean Sea. The railways of the island are known as FdS, 'Il Trenino Verde della Sardegna' – 'The Sardinian train in the wilderness'. This description hints at the considerable distances over which several of the narrow gauge lines run and the ruggedness of the terrain in which they were constructed. We shall look briefly at four of these branch lines.

Mandas-Arbatax

Some 2km north of Mandas, on the Cagliari-Sorgono line, a junction takes the Arbatax branch line to the north-east. The branch twists

and turns for almost its entire length of 159km. After Nurri the line really starts its climb into the exposed craggy hills covered in scrub and dwarf trees, with the train negotiating numerous sharp curves until the summit at 900 metres is reached, with a short tunnel between Seulo and Seni. Gorse bushes proliferate around the ever-changing mountain views as the train passes several remote and minor halts. The line was built with many linesmen's cottages, often sited at unguarded road crossings and at the very minor stations. At Seni station there are two loops and a two-road shed with a turntable and water facilities. The line then takes a convoluted course through rugged countryside with many outcrops and ravines, so that it can often be viewed across valleys in this sparsely populated region.

It is evident that Gairo station was formerly of some importance, having once been the junction for a 10km branch line south to Jerzu; there were previously double loops and water and turntable facilities for steam locomotives. From Gairo the single track once again contorts itself, then from Villagrande

The engine shed and disused turntable at the end of the line to the east coast port of Arbatax, where ferries from the Italian mainland make regular visits.

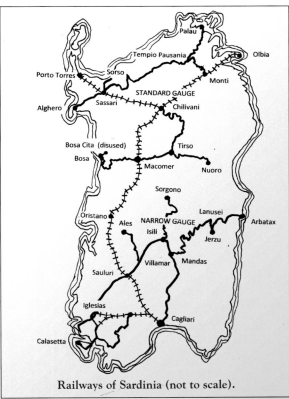

Railways of Sardinia (not to scale).

and its lake it at last starts its descent to Arbatax on the east coast. This is a busy port where ferry boats bring passengers from the mainland of Italy. Its station is similar to many others on the metre-gauge line, but with several long sidings serving the once busy freight traffic from the port.

The single-road engine shed and turntable remain, with a single track continuing to the dock area, where it passes over an opening metal girder bridge to a small dock; there the tracks fanned out and curved around the main harbour area, with a second station building overlooking the small dock.

Bosa-Macomer

Bosa is a small town on the west side of the island, and the line runs 49km east to the pleasant town of Macomer, which is an interchange station with the standard-gauge line running north-south. Bosa has two stations: the original terminus at Citta, near the town centre beside the road bridge over the River Temo, which is now disused, and a new EU-funded modern building at the estuary Marina station. Here there are several sidings with just a few freight wagons, but once again there is a goods shed and turntable.

Bosa's modern single-platform station is adjacent to the earlier Marina station and freight yard. A diesel-electric 'ADe' railcar is ready to leave on its return trip to Macomer up in the hills.

Leaving the Marina station, the train follows the shore for a short distance, then starts to climb up into the hills, reaching the high plateau at Tresnurages. It trundles through the rolling uplands and crosses over the standard-gauge line at Macomer, a major town and railway headquarters of the railway system. The run-in to the narrow-gauge station, and its attendant workshops and engine sheds, witnesses a mixture of ancient derelict coaches and wagons, and modern rolling stock. Intermixed with these are rusting steam locos and old railcars, and even an old hand-operated rail-mounted crane. Outside the workshops is

A small sleepy halt on the narrow-gauge line in the hills above Arbatax.

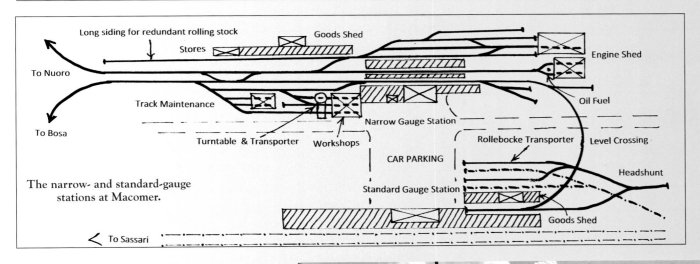

The narrow- and standard-gauge stations at Macomer.

Below: An 'Ade 93' diesel-electric railcar in the smart FdS grey and green livery crosses the Macomer main road towards the joint platform with the standard-gauge line. These railcars were built between 1995 and 1996 by ABB/ Tecnomasio.

a railway transporter and turntable, and a small siding for track maintenance vehicles.

There is a relatively new platform area at the end of the line, and beyond it a single track curves sharply right across the unguarded main road and becomes dual gauge as it enters the standard-gauge station. Here the narrow-gauge track runs into its own bay platform, connected to several dual-gauge sidings where interchange took place between the two gauges. Rollboke wheel sets were attached to the standard-gauge wagons for transit onto the narrow gauge; these were evidently used most on the Nuoro branch line, which struck out east from Macomer.

Below: Macomer is a major interchange station, and has a host of varied old and new rolling stock, with the latest blue and white livery seen on this elegant coach.

Above: Macomer narrow-gauge station is across the road from the standard-gauge facility, with a joint platform. At the workshops we see a remodelled 'Ade' railcar built in the 1950s, while on the left is a double-ended diesel-electric BB freight loco of the 6XX Series built by Breda, also in the 1950s.

Sassari-Alghero

The narrow-gauge branch line from the west coast town of Alghero to the inland rail hub town of Sassari is the shortest route of the four being considered, and also the only one to have been modernised. Alghero is an ancient walled town and port and is of considerable delight. The port now is devoted to pleasure craft but once handled freight traffic, with a single line extending from the town station into the dock area, crossing the main road from the north into the town. To reach the docks the track ran between houses, then opened out onto the quayside, but the line was partly lifted in 1988.

The 35km branch was opened on 1 April 1889 and was built by Sardinian Secondary Rail Roads (SFSS); 40% of the construction costs were met by local authorities. This rural line made its headquarters at Alghero, which today is very much a tourist destination, and the recent modernisation of the branch is no doubt due to the urbanisation around the old town, whose population has increased considerably. Alghero station is a 1960s concrete structure with two tracks serving an island platform. Other tracks serve a goods shed, and all have been modernised with electric colour-light signals. For the sparse passenger traffic, this does rather look like overkill. Modern Ferrosud DE railcars running as two units carry passengers to Sassari, where they are able to make connections with almost the entire island of Sardinia. These units are equipped with full 'cow-catchers' and have three lights at each end. They have two Fiat 165hp diesel engines that drive both bogies through four ABB 70kW electric motors. As with several other railcars, the local 'artists' have demonstrated their graffiti skills on the green upper panels and the white panels below the windows; green doors give access to the single-class passenger accommodation.

Along the line there is just one passing loop at Mamuntanas, some 25km from Sassari.

Sassari-Tempio Pausania-Palau

Tempio Pausania is an attractive major hill town on the Sassari to Palau line. From here north-west to the coastal port of Palau is 59km, and the line was opened in January 1932. It was also the terminus of the now-closed branch line running north from Monti, which had a standard-gauge station on the Sassari to Olbia line. The railway facilities at Tempio are on a grand scale, with the large station buildings housing the divisional offices and a popular bar!

Tempio station is at the summit of the line from Sassari and consists of four through loops with two sidings both north and south of the station. These are utilised for the storage of rolling stock, including several green-painted Bauchiero bogie coaches with end verandas, open wagons with end platforms for hand brakes, covered vans with low-pitched camber roofs, and vans with a brake-operator's lobby, all very characterful and full of interest. Also stored across from the platform were two rusting 2-6-0 tank engines built by Breda in 1914, their once unlined black livery relieved by red wheels with white rims, red coupling rods and buffer beams – now only a memory of their heyday.

Several sidings at Macomer still hold a wide collection of disused steam locomotives, coaches, rail cars and this hand-operated portable crane.

The single track leaves Sassari in a north-easterly direction and soon heads up into the hills, taking a winding course through Nulvi and on to Tempio, passing through two tunnels. The line comes into Tempio from the north and winds around the east side of the town before turning sharply into the station yard. Leaving Tempio the line runs through some spectacular scenery to Oddistru, then starts its descent towards Palau Town station.

Palau station has two loops, one of which has a turnout to the former single-road engine shed, with a reverse siding with a turntable. Attached to the two-storey station house is the goods shed and weighbridge, and there is a water tower between the two tracks. At the eastern end of the station the two loops come together and the line then descends 15 metres over a distance of 1km to terminate in a curved platform and simple buffer stop at Palau Marine station. A short reverse siding leads to a goods shed. From the buffer stop the line evidently once continued across the road and curved around to the edge of the quayside to deal with the freight traffic one received from the mainland. Palau is a bright and prosperous town with many new apartments and new developments, which seem to be just keeping this part of the railway running.

Above: An FS Class 245 Italian shunter is seen on the standard-gauge line at Macomer station, a junction with the narrow-gauge lines.

Above: Freight wagons are seen at Palau's town centre station, including this brakeman's vehicle. Beyond the station buildings a single line descends sharply for a short distance to the harbour station.

Left: A derelict 2-6-0 tank engine, built in 1931 by Breda, lies in the freight sidings at Tempio Pausania, the mid-way station to the east coast resort of Palau.

Part 2: Africa

Egypt

Travelling down the River Nile or staying in Luxor to visit the Temple of Karnak, the Valley of the Kings and other sites of antiquity is an unforgettable experience – probably one of the world's greatest open-air museums. Also not to be missed are the wonderful sunsets across the Nile, with the feluccas in silhouette.

Travellers to Luxor arrive by boat, road, plane and train, but it's the railway that is of real interest here, with its history and current usage.

The first railway to be constructed in Egypt was from Alexandria on the north coast to Cairo, a distance of 209km (130 miles), and was completed by 1856. It was built to the standard gauge of 4ft 8½in (1,435mm) and its Chief Engineer was Robert Stephenson. An extension was then constructed to Suez a few years before the Suez Canal was opened, for the transportation of Anglo-Indian freight between Cairo and Suez. This greatly reduced the distance to India, as ships could then sail down the Red Sea to the Indian Ocean instead of making the hazardous journey around the Cape of Good Hope.

The Nile Valley was tackled next, with a standard-gauge line from Cairo to Luxor (671km/419 miles), which was fully operational by 1898, with a line from Luxor to Aswan

A magical sunset over the Nile at Luxor.

(208km/130 miles) being completed shortly afterwards. This line was built to the narrow gauge of 3ft 6in (1,067mm), as it would form a part of Cecil Rhodes's grand scheme to have a continuous rail link from Cairo to the Cape of Good Hope. The narrower gauge would be compatible with other railways in the Sudan and eastern and southern Africa. However, this scheme failed to materialise and the line was converted to standard gauge in 1926 and absorbed into the state railway system.

Today Egyptian National Railways (ENR) serves Cairo and fans out across the Nile Delta to Alexandria and Port Said and down the Nile Valley to Luxor and Aswan.

Luxor is a thriving town reliant on tourism for its income, and many tourists, as well as local people, arrive by train. The station is an impressive building with a giant Egyptian eagle overlooking the town and towering colonnades at the entrance. Inside it is cool and spacious.

There are about six trains daily in each direction between Cairo and Aswan, with

Luxor railway station, an imposing building displaying the Egyptian eagle.

An Aswan-Cairo train hauled by an ENR Adtranz EMD DE2550 waits at Luxor.

a journey time of around 12 hours depending on the speed status of the train, as some are faster than others. Half an hour or so before the arrival of a train the station is buzzing with people waiting in anticipation. It appears that plenty of time is allowed at Luxor before the train departs, and the driver has time for a smoke.

The locomotives normally used on this route are Adtranz DE 2550 2,445hp diesel-electrics. They and the coaches are permanently covered in desert dust, which makes everything look a bit shabby. However, every so often a half-hearted attempt is made to clean the rolling stock by some railway employees, one working and two supervising. Oh well, it is 30 degrees C in the noonday sun!

A Plasser & Theurer 08-275 Unimat track tamping unit glides through Luxor.

The sugar cane railway network

Around the Luxor area can be seen a light rail network used to transport sugar cane from the fields to the local mills.

The first light railway network was constructed in 1869, with further systems added as new sugar mills were built along both sides of the Nile Valley. These railways provide efficient transport of the sugar cane from the large growing areas where roads are non-existent. There is more than 2200km (1,375 miles) of this narrow-gauge track, largely unchanged over the decades.

The track gauge chosen was 2 feet (610mm), and the rails are mounted by bolts and clamps on sleepers made of cold-formed metal plates 2mm (0.07in) thick placed about 1 metre (3ft 3½in) apart. The track is then laid directly on the earth without the use of ballast. The lengths of track are joined by fishplates with just one bolt at each rail end.

Small locomotives and specially made cane wagons transport the produce to the local mill, where a number of lines converge at junctions to wait for the cane to be unloaded. Most of the diesel locomotives are between 250hp and 350hp and are imported from Germany, Romania, Japan and Slovakia. The driver usually has an assistant to jump off and change the points along the way and check that any road crossings are clear.

The wagons are made to take the whole stalk

A narrow-gauge locomotive of about 250hp used to pull the loaded sugar cane wagons.

laid along the direction of travel. The wagons have two four-wheel bogie sets, and the wagon frame is 6 metres long by 1.5 metres wide (19ft 8in by 4ft 11in). They have side posts 150cm (5ft 11in) tall and three steel channels spaced equidistantly across the bottom of the frame to allow chains to be passed across for unloading by crane at the mill.

The sugar cane harvesting season is between December and June, when track, locomotives and wagons should be fully utilised and reliable.

With the vast network of lines converging on the mill, a strict timetable of working is used with three shifts over a 24-hour period. The number a wagons required for day and night working is assessed and specific times for arrival, unloading and departure are rigorously enforced. Failure of rolling stock is also taken into account.

In the fields, wagons are loaded manually or by tractor with a forked loading basket. A locomotive then collects the wagons from different parts of the farm to form a train going to the mill, which will leave at a predetermined time. Unloading the cane wagons at the mill is normally performed by passing chains under the cane and lifting out using a chain unloader.

Maintenance of most equipment is carried out in the closed season, between June and December, usually at a local depot, and any new wagons required are made at a manufacturing facility owned by the sugar company in Cairo. The rail tracks suffer badly from erosion, especially if they run alongside irrigation channels, and the sleepers rust and need replacement.

The cane is shipped to mills across the Nile by boat. As a boatload of cane could be from more than one farm, the farmer's identity is chalked on the side of each loaded bin, which holds about the same quantity of cane as a rail wagon. If a road trip is involved from the farm, before crossing the Nile to the mill, specially adapted craft transfer the tractors and carts across. Again, the carts hold the same amount of whole stalks as the rail wagons. Once at the mill dockside a crane transfers the cane to waiting narrow-gauge rail wagons, keeping each farmer's crop separate and identified. The train then moves to the mill where the cane is unloaded for processing.

The light railway networks still form the major transport link between the sugar cane fields and the mills. Compared to road transport they are more economical, reliable and have a low accident rate. Although their share of cane transportation has reduced over the years, the network sizes are very similar to a decade ago. The reduction in share is mainly due to the expansion of sugar cane fields outside of the areas served by the narrow-gauge rail networks and of course an increase in road haulage.

The sugar cane light railway networks should continue to serve the farmers and the industry for some time to come.

These fully loaded narrow-gauge sugar cane wagons are ready to be taken to the mill.

A typical boat on the Nile used to transport the farmers' sugar crop to the mill. Each stack is numbered for accurate weighing and to differentiate between two or three different farms.

The Cape Peninsula

Cape Town is an attractive city that nestles between the southern Atlantic Ocean and the foothills of Table Mountain. Its main station is the hub of four commuter networks and the terminus for long-distance inter-city trains.

Metrorail's Southern Line runs down the Indian Ocean side of the Cape Peninsula providing an efficient commuter service to the terminus at Simon's Town, the major South

A maintenance train of conveyor-connected wagons is being used to remove drifting sea sand from the single track built by Cecil Rhodes in 1890 to serve the Simon's Town naval base.

A Class 36 diesel was hauling the sand removal maintenance wagons.

African naval base. The line was opened by Cecil Rhodes on 1 December 1890 to transport essential supplies to the base, which was then occupied by the Royal Navy and was handed back to South Africa in 1957.

A short distance south of Simon's Town is Boulder Beach, home to a large colony of endangered African penguins. Many tourists are attracted to the site and enjoy walking among these lovable creatures.

From Fish Hoek to Simon's Town the line runs between the road and the beach, causing problems when high winds and storms from the Indian Ocean dump tons of sand onto the track, which has to be cleared immediately to avoid major disruption to train services. This is achieved using specially adapted wagons coupled together with conveyor belts to enable continuous loading of sand. If the sand is too deep it has to be cleared manually to avoid damage to trackside electric circuits.

In December 2009 a severe storm closed the line, which was unable to reopen until 21 February 2011 when sea walls, track and other railway infrastructures had been replaced.

At Dal Josafat there are several overgrown sidings that are the resting place of several large steam locomotives beside the elevated coaling plant, awaiting their fate.

Diesel locomotives stand under the overhead oil fuel lines at the large workshops at Dal Josafat, north-east of Cape Town.

Other Cape Town departures

A wonderful trip to experience, albeit an expensive one, is the five-star 'Blue Train', which leaves Cape Town and travels northwards to Pretoria, providing breathtaking views of the African subcontinent. The journey takes 27 hours and covers the 994 miles (1,600km) with organised stops and short trips for wine-tasting, etc. There are approximately four trips in each direction each month of the year.

There are also occasional steam- and electric-hauled tourist specials leaving Cape Town for various sightseeing trips with overnight sleeping in vintage carriage stock. A typical route takes the train to Worcester in the Western Cape area, where the overhead electric supply terminates, and the electric locomotive is exchanged for a steam or diesel locomotive to continue the journey to Ashton and onwards to the foothills of the Langeburg Mountains. If the train is steam-hauled it might be double-headed by a Class 19D 4-8-2 with a Beyer-Garratt 4-8-0+0-8-4 of the GMAM Class, each with an additional water tank wagon. Overnight stops are made and passengers can then relax and recount the day's activities and enjoy the food served up in the superb dining car. Continuing on this route the train passes through George,

In typically beautiful scenery there are river gorges to be crossed, as here with a Class 19D 4-8-2 and a Beyer-Garratt 4-8-2+2-8-4 of Class GEA of 1953 giving all their worth – just wonderful!

231 miles (3,719km) from Cape Town and the beginning of the famous 'Garden Route'. George was once a busy interchange for the branch line to the Little Karoo and Oudtshoorn, renowned for its ostrich farms, but the line closed in February 2007. In the heady days of steam George boasted a large marshalling yard and locomotive workshops with a short length of 2-foot-gauge tramway serving the coaling plant.

Top left: The 'Union Limited' heads out on the Oudtshoorn line into the 'Little Karoo' with a Class 19D leading the Beyer Garratt GEA and the obligatory water tank wagon.

Above and left: The double-headed 'Union Limited' storms up a grade, the two mighty 2ft 6in-gauge goliaths showing off, the epitome of glorious steam railways!

30

Class 26 4-8-4 No 3450 *Bethlehem* returns to Cape Town from Worcester hauling vintage clerestory coaches on a special train.

The 'Garden Route'

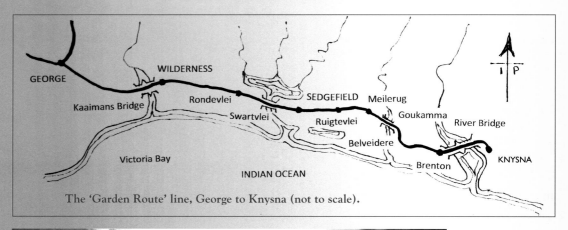

The 'Garden Route' line, George to Knysna (not to scale).

The 'Garden Route' is an area of coastline stretching from Mossel Bay, just south of George, eastwards to Storm River in the Eastern Cape. It is so called because of the verdant and ecologically diverse vegetation that is abundant, and it has numerous coastal lakes, lagoons and coral reefs.

The route from George drops 226 metres through the Outeniqua mountain range, negotiating several bridges and tunnels to reach sea level where it crosses the Kaaimans Viaduct, an attractive curved structure 689 feet (210m) long and 118 feet (36m) high, which crosses the mouth of the Kaaimans River to the small coastal town of Wilderness with its sand dunes and golden beach. It then closely follows the 'Garden Route' coastline together with the main N2 highway towards the terminus at Knysna, some 42 miles (67km) away. Construction of this stretch of line commenced in 1922 and it opened in 1928; it is reputed to be the most expensive railway line built in Africa.

On its way to Knysna the train passes through some glorious countryside and finally enters the outskirts over a long low bridge that spans the lagoon at the head of the estuary. There is then a short run seaward into the station, which is located in the heart of this most attractive town.

Within the station area are sidings mainly used for timber and refuse, waiting to be taken

The double-headed 'Union Limited' crosses the Kaaimans Bridge on the George-Knysna line. The sign at each end of the bridge instructs in several languages that 'Unauthorised persons not allowed on the bridge'.

to George for processing, and a turntable to turn the locomotive for its return journey.

During 1992 scheduled services ceased and the line was declared a preserved line for steam operations – the Outeniqua Choo Tjoe – run by Transnet Heritage Preservation. The locomotives most commonly used were Class 24 2-8-4s (built in 1948) and Class 19D 2-8-4s (built between 1937 and 1948), mainly constructed by the North British Locomotive Company in Glasgow.

Unfortunately, the operation closed down in 2007 after severe flood damage and it is not known whether the line will reopen in the future.

Right: Wilderness is a small settlement along the coast that boasts a good hotel and beach. Idling in the station, in full South African livery, is a Hunslet 0-4-0 diesel with just a minimum load!

Below right: At Sedgefield station two Class 19D 4-8-2s pass; on the left is No 2683 'Tootsie' from Knysna. Both were built in the 1940s by the North British Locomotive Co of Glasgow.

Left: 'Tootsie' is seen again filling up with water at a midway station before continuing on the 'Garden Route' along the coast to Knysna.

North-east South Africa

Not far from the Kruger National Park is Pilgrims Rest. This is a characterful old gold-mining town more typical of the North American 'wild west'. The South African gold rush was not on the scale of the Californian one, but nevertheless in 1873 gold was discovered near the town of Sabie on the Mpumalanga Escarpment. In that year the area was declared as a goldfield and by the end of the year there were 4,000 claims being worked by 1,500 men. The mine was finally closed in 1972. On the far side of a creek opposite the town is an embankment alongside the stream, which is part of the 3ft 6in-gauge single-track railway that was powered by overhead electric pylons still in existence.

Zimbabwe

At Victoria Falls station a freight train hauled by Zimbabwe Railways (NRZ) Co-Co diesel No 2112 will shortly cross over the spectacular Zambezi Bridge into Namibia. To the right is a large freight yard.

Victoria Falls

Another miniscule narrow-gauge railway catered for wealthy tourists visiting Victoria Falls, transporting them from their hotels to the falls, the wagons being pushed by locals. This was so that they could avoid meeting up with the noisy warthogs!

At the main station of Victoria Falls many freight trains stop before passing over the metal viaduct on their way to deliver fuel oil to Zambia and Zimbabwe. The single-platform station has numerous sidings where NRZ coaches and sometimes a Garratt locomotive may be seen.

Part 3: Asia

India

The Kalka-Shimla Railway

If visiting the Kalka-Shimla Railway, nestling in the foothills of the Himalayas, it is preferable to take the 'Shatabdi Express' from New Delhi, which covers the 170 miles (272km) northwards to Kalka in about 4 hours.

New Delhi station has 16 platforms, which accommodate 300 trains a day; it is the largest hub station with six major routes, handling some 360,000 passengers a day. The track is broad gauge, 5ft 6in (1,676.4mm), and the 6,000hp Co-Co electric locomotives of Class WAP5 are powerful enough to pull the long trains over the great distances. Power is supplied by a 25kV catenary network.

Leaving New Delhi and its somewhat squalid and overcrowded suburbs, the train passes through more remote agricultural areas where wild peacocks strut around and sari-clad women tend the fields – such a stark contrast to the capital!

Kalka is the terminus station in the foothills of the Himalayas where the broad-gauge main-line platforms are end-on to the narrow-gauge station. The huge buffer stops for the broad gauge were built by Ransome & Rapier of

Victoria station in Bombay (Mumbai) of the Great Indian Peninsula Line (GIPL) was built by the British in grand colonial style. *Ian Peaty*

Ipswich, Suffolk, and are still carrying out a splendid job after nearly a century.

The end-on platform has a canopy, shading the colourful narrow-gauge train of six coaches and the blue-and-cream-liveried Class ZDM-3 Bo-Bo diesel loco, with dual-direction cab. Leaving Kalka the little train first passes the modern workshops and engine shed, where sacred cows are prone to take a rest among the

huge diesel locos! It soon begins its climb into the hills, opening up superb vistas.

The 2ft 6in-gauge (762mm) railway opened for traffic on 9 November 1903 with a total distance of 60.3 miles (96.54km) with the intention of transporting Government officials and the army of the British Raj to a cooler area to work in the extremely hot summers that are normal in the plains of India; the cool

The broad-gauge Class GT46 MAC locomotives were built in the USA by General Motors in 2001. They are powerful Co-Co diesels of 4,000hp, and their livery matches that of the coaches.

The WDM-2 Class Co-Co locomotives are the workhorses of the Indian broad-gauge railways. They were built by the US firm Alco in 1962.

temperate climate of Shimla, at an altitude of 6,811 feet (2,076m), was clearly the prize. The rise of 4,659 feet (1,420m) necessitates a winding course for the single-track railway, passing over 864 bridges and through 102 tunnels with a ruling gradient of 1 in 33. The longest tunnel, at 1,251 yards (1,143.61m) is at Barog station, which is also used as a passing loop. Originally built as a private concern, the line was taken over by the Indian Government on 1 January 1906.

Among the many bridges and viaducts are two stone-built examples with multiple layers of arches; the highest of these is between Sonwara and Dharampur, which is on a curve and has five tiers. At Solan station there is a distillery cut into the steep hillside. It was formerly a brewery with a malthouse and kiln and was once served by two rail sidings covered by a canopy, which still advertises the former product! Several stations have water columns and British-style semaphore signals, and the renowned London Transport Underground station signs are replicated in India!

As the train climbs even higher at a slow 14mph (22km/h) on a continually winding course, hugging the wooded hillsides, it provides many opportunities to enjoy the spectacular

Probably the only steam monorail train running in the world can be seen at the
Delhi Railway Museum. It was built in 1907 by Orenstein & Koppel of Berlin.

Kalka station is the broad-gauge terminus in the foothills of the Himalayas,
and meets the narrow-gauge hill railway end-on. Class WAP-5 No 30263 is at
the pneumatic buffers built by Ransome & Rapier of Ipswich at the time of the
British Raj.

views through deodar cedars, oaks and maples.
The little train eventually arrives at its terminus
in Shimla after an unforgettable journey of 4½
hours.

Shimla station has one long platform that
can handle two trains, with scissor crossings
midway permitting the trains to be moved
independently. These are supervised by the
signal box, which overlooks the entire station,
perched on the steep outward edge of the
railway. Tucked between station buildings is a
turntable used for a railcar, whose duties are only

local. The original railcars were built in 1911
by the Drewery Car Co Ltd of London, with
17hp petrol engines, but these were replaced in
1932 by diesel-electric railcars that can carry up
to 14 passengers and run to the local station at
Springfield.

Shimla is a town built on a hill surmounted
by a very typical English parish church with
a square and surrounded by Edwardian-style
houses. Clinging to the very steep hillsides are

the bustling streets with shops and houses, and
many porters carrying goods on their shoulders.
In the town an ornate four-storey red and white
building was formerly the headquarters of the
North Western Railway, and today is shared
with the local military.

When the line opened, steam locomotives
of Class B were built by Sharp Stewart & Co
of Glasgow, similar to those still working on
the Darjeeling Railway. Hunslet and the North

At the narrow-gauge diesel shed at Kalka the foreman's sign above the wagon wheel exhorts 'Man's Greatest Invention, Keep It Moving' – nothing can beat that!

At Kalka's narrow-gauge workshops a sacred cow seems prepared to assist the powerful diesels in a little light shunting!

British Locomotive Co supplied two classes of locos, while in 1928 Kitson-Meyer provided articulated locomotives, although they were found to be unnecessarily powerful. In 1955 a German company supplied ZDM-1 Class diesel locomotives, and five years later Class 2, built by another German firm. Today two classes of diesel work the line, Class ZDM-3 built in 1970-82 by the Indian firm of Chittaranjan Locomotive Works, and a further six built at the at Central Railway Workshops in 2008-09.

Passenger coaches were originally four-wheeled, but since 1908 they have all been bogie coaches of two classes painted in various colours. There are several level sidings at Shimla for the coaches, and a two-road engine shed at the opposite end of the station.

It is gratifying to know that this unique narrow-gauge hill railway is designated a UNESCO Heritage site, together with India's other two hill railways, the Darjeeling and Nilgiri, both from the same era of British/Indian history.

Above left: This is one of the 864 bridges, some of spectacular design, on the narrow-gauge hill railway from the foothills of the Himalayas up to Shimla.

Above: This is Barog station viewed from the portal of the longest tunnel on the line, one of the 102 encountered. Note the precise white lining to the edges of the track ballast – this could only have been done by a military trained railwayman!

Left: A train enters Shimla station up the gradient, hauled by a ZDM-3 diesel-hydraulic locomotive, one of a class built between 1970 and 1982 at Chittaranjan Locomotive Works, with a later batch built in 2008-09 at the Central Railway Workshops.

Above: The end of the line at Shimla, with carriage sidings on the right and the diesel engine shed and workshop on the left. Diesel locomotive No 151 is ready for fuelling and will then take its train back down to Kalka. The fir trees cover the temperate hillsides all around Shimla.

This motor railcar for 14 passengers was built in 1927, and is used for special outings and local traffic between Shimla and Springfield.

Above: This is one of two Class B 0-4-0 saddle tank locomotives built in 1889 by Sharp Stewart & Co of Glasgow. They originally worked on the Shimla line, but are now better known for their appearances on the Darjeeling Mountain Railway.

Right: Has anyone seen our park bench…?

Sri Lanka

Known as Ceylon during the time of British occupation, it became Sri Lanka after independence in 1972, although the name Ceylon is still seen and used. It is a pear-shaped island just off the southern tip of India, measuring 270 miles (432km) from north to south and 140 miles (224km) across at its widest point. Its location means that it has wet and dry seasons, and tropical rain forest in the higher hills. Overall the island is very fertile and produces rice, vegetables, fruit, tea, rubber, coconut and spices, especially cinnamon, but is generally best-known for its tea plantations (Ceylon tea) in the hill country, which became the big cash crop from the 1870s. Prior to the tea plantations, coffee was grown in the hill country until plants were affected by the blight of the 1870s.

Sri Lanka is a beautiful island and its people are welcoming. It also has a busy railway network that is full of living history, but for this brief look at its railways we will confine our interests to the Main Line to Kandy and the Coast Line.

The railways of Sri Lanka.

Jaffna

(Northern lines closed Jan; 19, 1985)

Mannar

To be opened end of 2014

Vavuniya

(closed)   Medawachchiya Jnc

Trincomalee

Anuradhapura   Gal Oya Jnc;

Puttalam   Polonnaruwa

(closed)

Maho Jnc;   Batticaloa

Matale

Peigalawda Jnc;   Kandy

Peradeniya Jnc;

Ragama
Avissawella

Colombo   Nuwara Eliya   Badulla

Mount Lavinia   Nanu Oya

Bandarawela

Kalutara

Dodaniduwa   Hambantota

NEW EXTENSION   Completion due 2015

Galle   (Length 114.5 km)

Matara

Above: This former Class W1 diesel locomotive was built in 1969 by Henschel and was re-engineered in 1997 by Sri Lanka Railways. Reclassed as Class W3, the locomotives now have Caterpillar 3512 DITA engines with new transmission and hydro-dynamic braking.

Right: An Indian-built Class M8 2,600hp Co-Co diesel-electric locomotive heads towards Anuradhapura on the Northern Line.

The Main Line

As the roads into the hill country were inadequate at that time for the transportation of coffee, and bullock carts were slow and not plentiful, pressure mounted for the introduction of a railway line from Colombo, on the coast, to Kandy, then into the upper hill country to Nawalapitiya, Nanu Oya and Bandarawela. After several false starts, the Colombo to Kandy line was opened in 1867, to Nawalapitiya in 1874 and Bandarawela by 1895. This is known as the Main Line, and today has a total track length of 181 miles from Colombo to the end of the line at Badulla.

The single track was laid to a 5ft 6ins (1,676.4mm) broad gauge, and it was, and still is, the highest broad-gauge line to be found anywhere, reaching an altitude of 6,226 feet (2,019m). The track was doubled between Colombo Fort and Rambukkana by 1926, then a third running track had been laid from Colombo Fort to Ragama by 1997, as traffic became heavier.

Needless to say, the original line was built during the British rule of Ceylon at the time of Queen Victoria and became the start of the Ceylon Government Railway. Most of the infrastructure for the line was of British manufacture and the first steam locomotive arrived on the island in January 1864; it was a 4-4-0, numbered 1 and named *Leopold*, built by Stephenson as No 1263.

A typical country station on the Main Line.

A Class M6 locomotive pulls into Ella with a down train to Nanu Oya on the Main Line from Colombo Fort to Bandarawela.

The starting point for the Main Line is Colombo Fort, where the train makes its way towards Kandy, Sri Lanka's second city. Kandy nestles in the mountains of the hill country, surrounded by green and succulent tropical forest, and is a centre for traditional arts, crafts and religious pageantry.

Lake Kandy is the city's scenic area, with the Temple of the Tooth and Royal Palace at the water's edge. Just outside the city limits is the Peradeniya Botanical Gardens, 147 acres of beautiful trees and plants. At weekends it is a traditional haunt of courting couples, who hide away behind the giant trees, as they are normally expected to behave properly at all times in public. If they are seen by the staff patrolling the gardens they blow a whistle to flush them out!

Kandy station is the terminus for both the Colombo and Badulla trains on the Main Line. It also serves the trains to Matale. Trains for either Colombo or Badulla depart the same way as they arrive, while Platform 1 has a through line that runs by the side of the main station building, crosses the station road via a crude level crossing and heads for Matale.

The original station, opened in 1867, is long gone and the current building dates from the 1960s and is able to accommodate the increase in passengers and provide better ticketing facilities. The view from the station towards Peradeniya Junction provides a nostalgic display of signals on gantries and posts, while the Kandy

Above right: A Class M6 pulls the 'Intercity Express' up the steady grade high into the tea country to Nanu Oya.

Right: A 1,425hp Class M2 locomotive, built by General Motors, approaches Kandy station with the Colombo-Kandy express. Note the wonderful array of semaphore signals from the Victorian era, still in good working order.

A Class M7 is ready to leave Platform 1 at Kandy for Matale.

This is the main signal box on the end of Kandy station. Everything is still in good working order after nearly 150 years.

signal cabin is a sight to behold. It is all original and the signal team are proud to be working there, keeping everything in immaculate condition, with the brass sparkling.

A turntable still occupies a corner of the station yard, but sadly has not been used since the days of steam.

On departing from Kandy the line becomes a single track towards Peradeniya Junction. This is a triangular junction with platforms on each side; from Kandy trains go left to the upper hill country or right towards Colombo. The station is one of the oldest in Sri Lanka, opened in 1867 when the Main Line was extended to Kandy. At that time it was not a junction, but became so in 1873 when the Main Line was extended to Gampola on its way up to

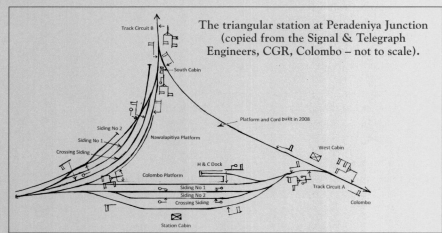

The triangular station at Peradeniya Junction (copied from the Signal & Telegraph Engineers, CGR, Colombo – not to scale).

Track Circuit B

South Cabin

Siding No 2

Siding No 1

Crossing Siding

Nawalapitiya Platform

Platform and Cord built in 2008

West Cabin

H & C Dock

Colombo Platform

Siding No 1

Track Circuit A

Siding No 2

Crossing Siding

Colombo

Station Cabin

Nanu Oya. At that time it was a 'Y' junction, with trains either from Kandy going either to Gampola or Colombo. It was not until 2008 that the short connecting line was constructed by Sri Lanka Railways from the Colombo line to the Nanu Oya line, together with a third platform, so that trains from Colombo to Badulla could continue into the upper hill country and avoid reversal at Kandy.

Inside the station office is a Tyer's tablet machine for single-line working, with a couple of hoops and pouches for the tablets. The ticket office is truly dated and totally manual, and the staff are friendly and helpful.

Peradeniya Junction boasts three signal cabins, one at the west extremity on the Colombo line, one at the southern extremity on the Badulla line, and the Station cabin for the short stretch to Kandy.

The distance from Peradeniya Junction to Nanu Oyu on the 'Inter City Express' is 57.63 miles (92.21km), which is covered at an average speed of 16.5mph (26.3km/h), but the trip is well worth every minute, especially if there is a First Class observation coach at the rear of the train. This is a unique trip along the single track, gradually climbing through the beautiful lush, green country, passing through small towns and eventually reaching the tea plantations near Nanu Oya.

Bandarawela is 32½ miles (52.1km) beyond Nanu Oya and just over halfway to Badulla. The station was open for use in 1894, and is a Victorian museum in itself, most of it now unused and the yard area showing the

unfortunate signs of neglect now that the steam era has gone. But what remains is of great interest as it still looks very serviceable. There is a two-road engine shed with pits and raised walkways and a water tower right outside, while the Victorian turntable was made by Cowans Sheldon of Carlisle in 1893. All that is needed to complete the scene is a locomotive in steam!

The line from Peradeniya to Badulla is single track with British-style semaphore signalling and tablet control. The Tyer's electric tablet room in Bandarawela station is in pristine condition, looking the same as it did 100 years ago.

Ella is the next station towards Badulla, a very quiet and beautiful location in the middle of tropical forest at an altitude of 3,416 feet (1,041m). It has a small goods shed, a hand-operated crane for heavier packages, and a water tower on a tall brick plinth; none of which are now in use.

Just around the curve at the end of the platform is an interesting and somewhat amusing sight. Perched on the crest of a fairly high hill, a little further down the line, is a semaphore stop signal for the up line. The line twists and turns as it ascends from Badulla, and with hills and steep cuttings so a signal would be difficult to locate in the correct place to be seen by the train crew.

The Uda Pussellawa Railway

Before leaving the hill country it is appropriate to mention the Uda Pussellawa Railway (UPR).

A number of tea-growers favoured the higher areas around Nuwara Eliya, but the nearest railway station was Nanu Oya on the Main Line. The roads were at least difficult and at worst impossible to navigate, and a narrow-gauge 2ft 6in (762mm) line was constructed through this difficult terrain.

The distance between Nanu Oya and Nuwara Eliya was 6½ miles (10.4km), and the line rose from 5,291 feet (1,612m) to 6,198 feet (1,888m). It then continued on to Kandapola at an altitude of 6,316 feet (1,925m), making that the highest station in Sri Lanka. The railway opened for commercial and passenger business in December 1903.

The locomotives used on the line were four Sharp Stewart L1 0-4-2T tanks, Nos 4822 to 4825, and a Beyer-Garratt 2-4-0+0-4-2T.

Unfortunately the line proved uneconomical and was closed to passenger traffic by 1940, and completely by August 1948.

Other broad-gauge lines and branches then followed the Main Line: the Matale line, the Northern line, the Batticaloa and Trincomalee lines, the Talaimannar line, the Puttalam line, the Coast Line and the Kelani Valley line (mixed gauge 2ft 6in/5ft 6in).

The Coast Line

Hang on tight! A commuter train calls at Mount Lavinia, a few miles outside Colombo on the Coast Line.

A Henschel-built Class M6 1,650hp locomotive heads for Colombo Fort station along the Coast Line.

The Coast Line runs along the south-west coast from Colombo Fort station to Sri Lanka's third city, Galle, 71 miles (114km) away. Galle, situated in the bottom south-west corner of the island, is a terminus station with a branch to Matara, another 27 miles (43km) distant. For most part the line runs just back from the sea and has no noticeable gradients, although a number of bridges cross rivers that meet the sea. This coast is quite heavily populated with endless villages and a large number of hotel complexes stretching down to Matara.

Located 8.2 miles (13km) south of Colombo is Mount Lavinia station, which is adjacent to the Mount Lavinia Hotel, once the residence of the Governor at the time of British rule. From Colombo to Panadura the line is double track, then becomes single track. At Mount Lavinia it expands to four tracks and three platforms, with an island platform serving both the centre up and down lines. For most of the route the line is visible from the road and beaches, but runs in a cutting as it passes the Mount Lavinia Hotel.

As the line continues towards Galle, the road and railway run alongside the Indian Ocean, giving the photographer good opportunities for railway photos.

Galle is a very engaging town that dates back to the time of the Dutch settlers. The old fort, with its imposing walls, dates back to 1684. In the town there are a myriad of renovated Dutch and English colonial properties, mainly given over to tourism in one way or another. Outside the fort the town is very Asian, with its station just a couple of minutes walk away.

Galle suffered badly at the time of the tsunami in December 2004. The giant wave went through the town and over the top of the station, causing great damage and many deaths. A Victorian prison adjacent to the station was, however, untouched; it was so well built that it withstood the force of the wave, and the windows were so small that the ingress of sea water was minimal and no prisoners lost their lives. Nevertheless, the tsunami was also the cause of the world's worst railway disaster between Galle and Beruwala. After the first wave hit land the local population tried to flee the area as quickly as possible, and it is believed that around 1,000 people managed to jump aboard the train (No 50) that was already carrying around 1,500 passengers. The second wave was larger and swept the whole train off the track, sending the coaches rolling over and over up to five times and ending up 150 metres (164 yards) further inland. Around 1,700 people died. The train was being pulled by Class M2a No 591 *Manitoba*. A memorial has subsequently been built at Telwatte, the exact location of the

An unusual photo of a Class M6 and a Class M4 approaching Lavinia running side-by-side on the bi-directional section of track towards Matale on the Coast Line.

A Brush Bagnall 1,000hp Class M7 locomotive leaves Mount Lavinia with an up train for Colombo Fort. Sixteen of these locomotives were imported in 1981 to coincide with the Queen's visit to the island.

disaster; it graphically depicts the tragic events showing the human suffering, the coaches and the locomotive.

Galle station and yard exhibit all the magnificent history of the late-Victorian railway builders, although like most of Sri Lankan stations most of the equipment required at the time for steam-hauled trains now lies unused, suffering the ravages of time and the tropical vegetation.

Galle is a terminus and trains have to depart in the same direction as they arrived. They also leave here for Matara, further round the coast in an easterly direction. The Galle-Matala extension was opened in 1895. Matara is a busy commercial coastal town and is currently the end of the Coastal Line.

However, the Coast Line is currently being extended, in stages, around the southern coast to the expanding Kataragama Harbour, a total of 71½ miles (114.5km) of single track, to improve transport between Kataragama and Columbo and its airport.

A total of 14 1,750hp Class M4 locomotives, built by Alco Bombardier at the Montreal Loco Works, were imported from 1975 onwards. This one is seen on the Coast Line heading for Matara.

Sunset across the Indian Ocean at Galle.

Left: A 530hp Y Class Hunslet diesel-hydraulic shunter is at work in Galle station yard.

Right: The Tsunami Monument at Telwatte on the Coast Line is dedicated to all those who were killed when in December 2004 a tidal wave swept an entire train off the track and into the tropical forest beyond.

Thailand, previously the Kingdom of Siam, has a long history dating back a thousand years and its exotic stupas (Buddhist shrines) and temples are testament to this gentle and beautiful country. It is the land of smiles, which is not surprising, as it has so much going for it, with its happy people who enjoy a standard of living above that of much of Asia, a mixture of tropical and lush countryside and, of course, Thai food. However, there is a darker side to the country's recent history when, as a neutral country, it was invaded by the Japanese. Evidence of this sad period is very apparent with the Allied graveyard and railway relics at Kanchanaburi, including the steel truss girder railway bridge over the river and immortalised in David Lean's 1957 film *The Bridge on the River Kwai*, starring Alec Guinness. This railway became known as the 'death railway'.

Railway interest in the country began in 1887-88 when a British contractor was commissioned by the Siam Government to survey and build a railway line from Bangkok, the present capital, to Ayutthaya, the former inland royal city and capital. A second line then followed from Ayutt to Lopburi, then continued northward to Lampang and Lamphun, terminating at Chiang Mai in the far northern mountains, which was the former capital of the northern kingdom.

Since those early days of British influence a

Bangkok's main station, Hua Lamphong, is an impressive structure built in the Italian renaissance style. Opened in June 1916, it has 14 platforms and serves 60,000 passengers every day with 130 trains of the State Railways of Thailand.

number of lines have been constructed, fanning out mainly from Bangkok's principal station, Hua Lamphong, to most parts of the country. There are five major lines and all have branches to provide maximum railway access for the Thai people. Lines are mainly single track and metre gauge, using the electronic token system. They are the Northern, North-eastern, Southern, Eastern and Maeklong Lines.

At Bangkok's Hua Lamphong station there is a shrine commemorating the founding of the Royal State Railway of Siam (RSR) by King Chulalongkorn in 1896; it was he who was popularised in the film *The King and I*. In 1951 the name was changed to State Railways of Thailand (SRT).

Top right: Alstom AD24C No 4420, built in 1985, is on shunting duty at the end of the platform at Bangkok.

Right: Class THN DMU No 1104, built in 1983, leaves Bangkok yard to make its way into Hua Lamphong station for a local service.

Southern Line: The Burma Railway

One of the routes on the Southern Line terminates at Kanchanaburi, but occasional trains continue the short distance to rumble over the Kwai Bridge, following the river's rambling course as far as Nam Tok station, which is well short of the Burmese border. Along this spectacular route the train carefully negotiates the famous timber trestle bridges built against the vertical cliffs and supported by large timber props into the edge of the river. The line and the bridges were built by Allied soldiers who were prisoners of the Japanese Imperial Army when they invaded Thailand during the Second World War. They worked and lived in the most appalling conditions and died in their thousands. The original line was 258 miles (415km) long between Ban Pong in Thailand and its termination in Burma.

At Kanchanaburi there are static locomotives and a road/rail truck used by the Japanese in the railway's construction. The renowned Kwai railway bridge is a replacement for the one bombed by the Allies.

Today the line is a living monument to the thousands of prisoners who died on the Burma Railway during those terrible wartime years.

Below: On permanent display by River Kwai bridge and used on the Burma Railway is ex-Japan Railways 2-6-0 No C5623, built by Kisha Seizo in 1936, then put into service with SRT after the war as No 719. It was put on display in 1977.

Below: Looking across today's Kwai Bridge towards Burma.

Northern Line: from Chiang Mai

Left: Thai steam locomotive No 340, a 2-8-0 built in 1912 by SLM Winterthur, Switzerland, is on display outside Chiang Mai station. It was originally in service with the Rhatische Bahn (RhB) on its metre-gauge network as No 118.

Top right: At Chiang Mai station, on the left is Daewoo Class APD 60 DMU No 2542 built in 1996, ready to leave on the 470-mile (751km) journey to Bangkok. On the right is a local DMU, Class THN (Tokyu, Hitachi, Nippon, Sharyo) No 1123 built in 1983.

Right: A closer view of Daewoo DMU No 2542 before it leaves on the somewhat arduous 13-hour journey to Bangkok.

The single-track line south from Chiang Mai terminus passes through a mixture of tropical and lush countryside on its 470-miles (751km) journey towards Bangkok. The preferred rolling stock appears to be three-coach DMUs, built in 1995 by Daewoo of South Korea. These have seen better days and are not without breakdowns. The level plains are devoted to rice-growing, and Thailand is one of the few countries to export the grain. The interesting but rather uncomfortable journey takes about 13 hours and arrival in Bangkok's Hua Lamphong station is most welcome!

Eastern Line from Makkasan

Makkasan station in Bangkok is full of interest, as here is located a large locomotive workshop and storage sidings for redundant steam locomotives. The many sidings are connected at the workshops by a traverser. A branch line for freight goes to the port area and to the Bang Chak oil refinery, with regular trains of oil tank wagons in both directions. At one point, in front of Makkasan station, the train emerges 'out of the bushes' with its numerous wagons, crosses a very noisy and busy road junction where the single-line token is exchanged, then disappears 'into the bushes' the other side! Above all this hive of activity and parallel with the double track in the station is the elevated and newly completed city terminus of the Bangkok Airport Transit, running on concrete viaducts and providing great views of the sprawling city.

Left: Alstom AD24C No 4152 leaves Makkasan station with a Bangkok-bound train. The concrete structure high above carries the new high-speed airport rail link.

Right: Makkasan is also the main works for the State Railways of Thailand and has a number of old steam locomotives stored around the premises. This is three-cylinder 4-6-2 No 278 built by Hanomag of Germany in 1929.

Malaysia

The first short 8-mile (13km) railway line under British colonial rule was opened in 1885 to move tin to a coastal port, and several others followed during the next 15 years. In 1906 Frank Swettenham amalgamated all the lines into the Federated Malay States Railway (FMS), which became Keretapi Tanah Melayu (Malaysian State Railways – KTM) in 1962.

The international express from Bangkok on the Southern Line crosses the Thai/Malaysian border to the international station of Butterworth. KTM has also adopted the metre gauge as standard to allow continuous running between the two countries. Fast and local trains then run along the west coast line to Penang, Ipoh and Kuala Lumpur, then south to cross the Johor Causeway into Singapore, a total distance of 719 miles (1,151km).

Kuala Lumpur is a modern city with many skyscrapers and landscaped highways. On the outskirts there is the Anchor-Guinness brewery, which has a

Left: Malay State Railways (KTM) Chinese-built Class 29 3,450hp diesel locomotive No 29116 is seen in Ipoh yard.

Below: Kuala Lumpur station was designed in a mixed Anglo-Eastern style by British architect Arthur Benison Hubback, and opened in 1910. It has two side platforms, a middle island platform and four running lines, and handles mainly commuter services. The main modern KL Sentral terminus is now a short distance up the line.

rail connection to the narrow-gauge main line. Guinness stout is popular in Malaysia and Singapore, which receive supplies from the brewery by rail.

Kuala Lumpur (KL) also has a 5½-mile (8.6km) elevated railway, utilising the monorail principle, which winds its way around the high buildings in a spectacular way. The railcars were built in Malaysia by Bhutan Malaysia. KL also boasts a very efficient light transit system with automatic

ticketing and fast, clean railcars. The original, very grand white station with its many minarets, built in 1910, is now used only for suburban traffic, while long-distance trains use the modern Sentral station just a short distance up the line.

Travelling further south from KL there is a considerable amount of railway construction work in hand to increase the number of parallel tracks and generally improve the journey between KL and Singapore. It is hoped that a high-speed line will be built in the near future to reduce the journey time from the present leisurely 6 hours to 90 minutes!

KTM is constantly modernising and it

Above: The KTM Class 82 three-car EMUs came into service from 1996, and are used on commuter routes out of KL. They use 25kV/50Hz overhead electrification. This unit, standing at the commuter platform inside the original KL station, is on the Batu Caves-Port Klang route.

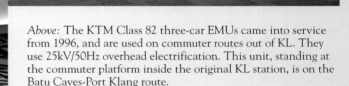

Left: KL has a monorail transit system running through the city between the Sentral station and Titiwangsa, a distance of 5½ miles (8.6km) serving 11 stations. It is a Thales Sel/ Trac straddle beam system with rubber tyre drive. Power is transmitted by external 750V DC pick-up rails.

shows in the quality of the trains, stations and increasing overhead electrification. German-built Class 26 diesel locomotives for passenger work are liveried in grey with blue, yellow and red bands, while the Chinese-built Class 29 freight locos are known as 'blue tigers', being dark blue with a white band. China has recently constructed locomotive workshops in Malaysia to build up to 150 new trains every year from 2014.

All this modernisation and railway construction is very much the ethos of this very modern Asian country, looking forward to the future.

Above: Class T 0-6-2T No 321.01 was built by Bagnall in 1927 and shipped to the Malay States in 1929. It worked mainly in Singapore and is now a permanent display at the National Museum in KL.

Left: Class 22 diesel No 22102 was built by a consortium of English Electric, AEI and Metro-Cammell in Birmingham, UK, in 1971 for KTM main-line service. It is also displayed at the National Museum in KL.

Guyana

The British influence has been felt around the world, as one would expect, especially in the old Commonwealth colonies. In the entire continent of South America, the very first railway was built in the only British colony, British Guiana, situated on the north-east coast and surrounded to the north-west by Venezuela, to the south by Brazil, and to the east by Surinam (Dutch Guiana). The nearest British colony was Trinidad, some 400 miles north in the Atlantic Ocean, which also had its own railway system, although built at a later date. British Guiana, once referred to as 'BG', is now a republic called Guyana. It consists of some 83,000 square miles with a mixed population of 767,000 people divided between chiefly East Indians, then those of African descent, Portuguese and North European, Chinese and the old indigenous tribes of Amerindians.

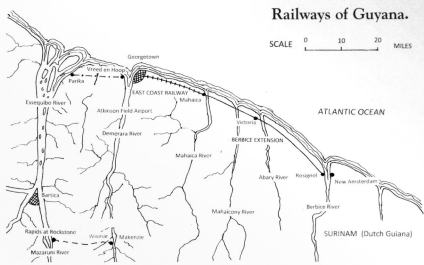

Railways of Guyana.

Guyana is a land of diverse geography that includes mountain ranges, tropical jungle and coastal plains. One of the rivers that flows out to the Atlantic on Guyana's eastern coastal plain is the Demerara, which gives its name to the renowned brown sugar. It was the need to transport this valuable commodity quickly and efficiently to Georgetown Docks, on the Demerara River, for export that became the driving force behind the building of the railway.

This Sharp Stewart 0-6-0 saddle tank was one of three dating back to the 1850s, all with local fauna names such as *Mosquito*, *Sandfly* and *Firefly*.

Above: Ancient rolling stock is being shunted at Georgetown freight yard on the public East Coast Railway in 1955, watched by a Scots laddie.

Below: A platoon of Black Watch soldiers load a jeep at Belem station for a trip along the coast to the Dutch Guiana (Surinam) border at Rosignol.

Top right: An ex-Bermuda Railway railcar, with troops on board, is ready to propel a platform truck, carrying a jeep, for a trip through the jungle.

The Demerara Railway

A Bill was passed in July 1846 authorising the construction of the East Coast Line (Demerara Railway) from Georgetown, running south to Rosignol on the Berbice River, near the border with Surinam. The Demerara Sugar Company was the major financier, together with a number of other sugar estates. John Bradshaw Sharples was the builder and the standard-gauge, single-track line opened on 3 November 1848, and was then extended in stages to complete the 60½ miles (97.4km) to Rosignol by 1897. Apart from the freight, which was mainly sugar, there was a passenger service of two trains a day to Plaisance, a small community about 6 miles (9.6km) south of Georgetown. This service continued until 1 January 1922 when, after financial problems, it was sold to the Colonial Transport Department.

The route travelled along level ground protected from the sea by high banks, but as sugar requires much water there were numerous irrigation dykes and canals to be crossed by the railway with several substantial steel bridges. In 1922 Dorman Long & Co Ltd supplied 70lb flat-bottom rails, which included the replacement of rails at several street level crossings in Georgetown up to the Lamaha Street terminus, which is now a bus depot.

Around 1948 the standard-gauge Bermuda Railway closed and its entire rolling stock and ancillary equipment was sold to BG for £86,000

to replace and support the ageing Demerara Railway.

The railway was equipped with British-built steam locomotives, with three in 1847 named *Mosquito*, *Sandfly* and *Firefly*, all very appropriate names of the local fauna. In 1863 two more were supplied, named *Alexandra* and *Victoria*. With these ancient steamers requiring increased maintenance, in the early 1950s orders were placed with the Vulcan Foundry of Newton-le-Willows for a 200hp 0-6-0 diesel-mechanical loco, with a further order for a similar one. A survey in 1955 revealed that there were seven steam locomotives, two diesel locomotives, petrol tractors for shunting, four petrol railcars, 55 passenger coaches, 87 covered vans, 344 open wagons, and nine rice vans. All the steam locomotives used imported coal, as it was established that bagasse, the residue of sugar production, and also local peat, were not suitable fuels. The line was eventually closed in 1972.

The Demerara - Essequibo Railway

The Demerara-Essequibo Railway also started operations in 1848 from its terminus in Vreeden Hoop, which was the settlement opposite Georgetown on the Demerara River. It was built to the narrow gauge of 3ft 6in (1,066.8mm) and ran 19 miles (30.4km) up the east coast to Parika on the Essequibo River. It had nine stations and only one major steel bridge over the Boeraseric River. This little railway closed in 1974, outlasting the main standard-gauge Demerara Railway by two years. Steam locomotion was used but details are poorly recorded, although an outside-cylinder loco with a four-wheeled tender and a 'balloon' spark-arrester chimney is known to have been used in the railway's construction.

After elections in 1953 a constitutional crisis arose when the PPP Party, who were communist sympathisers, won 18 of the 24 seats in the House of Assembly, persuading the Governor to invoke direct rule until 1957. The British Army were flown in to keep the peace and made use of the railways to transport their equipment.

Busy activity at a sugar mill, with steel barges loaded with cut cane from the many canals about to be unloaded onto diesel-hauled trains to travel to the mill for processing.

American diesel locomotive No 2040 at the Bauxite Mining Museum with the control cabin (signal box) behind, now out of use.

Bauxite railways

Several private railway networks of various gauges were built for bauxite mining and timber companies. One such bauxite line was the Mackenzie Three Friends, which is thought to have been of 2ft 6in (762mm) gauge and to have closed in the 1950s. A further railway in the Mackenzie district would appear to have been of 3-foot (304.8mm) gauge running to the Ituni Township from the mining area; operated by modern diesel locos it carried the bauxite ore in tipper wagons for loading into ships docked on the Demerara River.

Georgetown Electric Tramway

In Georgetown, the elegant colonial capital, a horse-drawn tramway was built in the early 1900s to the standard gauge. It was electrified by the 1920s by the Demerara Electric Co of Montreal, Canada. Fourteen electric trams were ordered from the St Louis Car Co of Missouri, USA. The tramway was 14 miles (22.4km) in length, even traversing the high protective banks on the coast. The life of the tramway was 27 years, closing in February 1930.

Cuba

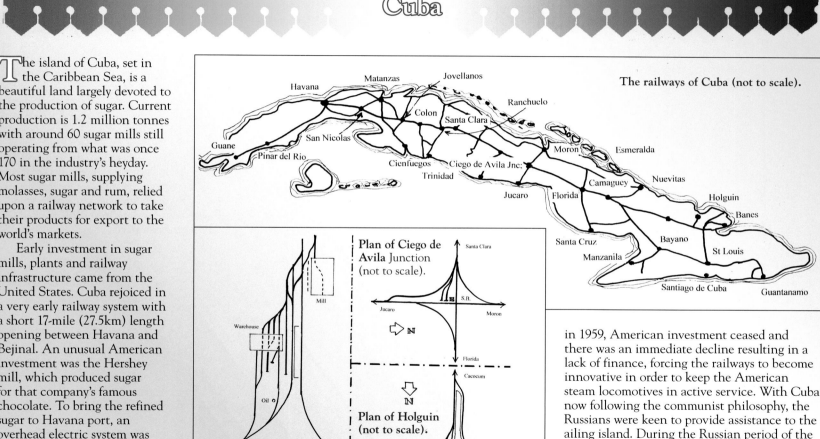

The railways of Cuba (not to scale).

Plan of Rafael Freyre sugar mill (not to scale).

Plan of Ciego de Avila Junction (not to scale).

Plan of Holguin (not to scale).

The island of Cuba, set in the Caribbean Sea, is a beautiful land largely devoted to the production of sugar. Current production is 1.2 million tonnes with around 60 sugar mills still operating from what was once 170 in the industry's heyday. Most sugar mills, supplying molasses, sugar and rum, relied upon a railway network to take their products for export to the world's markets.

Early investment in sugar mills, plants and railway infrastructure came from the United States. Cuba rejoiced in a very early railway system with a short 17-mile (27.5km) length opening between Havana and Bejinal. An unusual American investment was the Hershey mill, which produced sugar for that company's famous chocolate. To bring the refined sugar to Havana port, an overhead electric system was installed on the private railway in 1916.

After the political problems in 1959, American investment ceased and there was an immediate decline resulting in a lack of finance, forcing the railways to become innovative in order to keep the American steam locomotives in active service. With Cuba now following the communist philosophy, the Russians were keen to provide assistance to the ailing island. During the Russian period of the 1970s a new main line running east to west was built, with a few colour-light signals and a few manned signal boxes at junctions. Both

Above: General Electric Class B-B 120 No 29, built in 1925, worked on the American Hershey Railway (of chocolate fame) from its Mantanzas sugar mill to the coast. This fine electric locomotive is now on view at Havana's Cristina station.

Below: The Moron workshops are used to service American-built diesels such as this Class 38 Bo-Bo No 38161, which is in the livery of locomotives that only work the sugar trade trains.

standard and narrow gauges are used. However, train control is almost exclusively by phone, on mainly single track, the train guard relaying written instructions to the driver. Russian interest ceased in 1991, leaving the Cubans to fend for themselves with little or no public finance.

On the Russian-built line in the centre of the island is Ciego de Avila station with its four-way junction. A little to the east is Camaguey, another junction, with an American-style roundhouse engine shed, complete with a turntable feeding 20 tracks, and a locomotive traverser. This is where all the 270 Russian diesel locomotives are serviced.

From Ciego de Avila Junction a line heads north to Moron, where it connects with an older coastal main line. At Moron there is another major workshop, which is designated for the repair of the Canadian and sugar mill fleet of diesels and is the base for the breakdown train, with its heavy-duty American crane. At the

Lenin Park in Havana was built by the Russians, but here an American Baldwin 2-6-0 locomotive crosses a new concrete bridge, with the original branch-line truss girder bridge abandoned in the foreground.

Patria O Muerte sugar mill there is an excellent collection of preserved American steam locomotives.

From another multiple junction at Ranchuelo, a southbound branch line terminates at Cienfuegas and nearby is the Esteban Hernandez sugar mill, with a 2ft 6in-gauge line to the sugar cane fields and a standard-gauge connecting line. At one point the two gauges cross on the level, controlled by a dual-aspect semaphore signal. There is a another railway museum at the Jose Smith Comas mill, where the railway runs down the middle of town and passes under an ornate archway. The adjacent rail sidings have many tank and cane-carrying wagons, which include some built in Iran. On the opposite side to the terminus platforms is a rum factory, which is also connected by its own rail line.

On the south-eastern seaboard is the renowned American military base of Guantanamo, with a railway line extending 675 miles (1,080km) to the west at Guana. There are numerous short branch lines leaving the main line, radiating out to both north and south coasts serving many sugar mills. There are passenger services on the major lines that connect with most towns. South of Holguin, to the east, is the renowned Rafael Freyre sugar mill set in beautiful limestone hills and lush

Right: Seen from a hill overlooking the spectacular countryside, a Baldwin 2-8-0, built in 1911, hauls sugar cane wagons from the Rafael Freyre mill.

Above: In a typical scene at a loading siding on the edge of a sugar plantation, high-sided rail wagons are ready for collection to be taken to a central sugar-processing mill.

Above: Everything stops for schoolchildren and the horse and cart as they cross the main street, so American Vulcan 2-8-0 No 1728, built in 1920, has to wait. This is a common sight with the railway running down the middle of a village street.

plantations, from where the railway takes the finished products to other working mills.

In the centre of Havana is the now closed Cristina station, which is an excellent railway museum. Havana is now a World Heritage site and rejoices in Spanish-style architecture painted in lovely pastel shades, all enhanced by the many American streamlined and colourful cars of the 1950s. These old vehicles are kept in running order by innovation and loving care. The Russian contribution is the large public park 'Parque

Above: No 1728 continues its journey down another village street with typical houses and church.

Left: A short wait at a station allows the driver of the 2-8-0 to oil up his steed. Note the 'modern' concrete station canopy to give some protection from the heat to a few passengers.

Left: Camaguey diesel workshops are used to service Russian-built locomotives in the former American-built roundhouse for steam locomotives, with the turntable serving 20 tracks.

Below: At Esteban Hernandez sugar mill, a Che Guevara sign overlooks the 2ft 6in-gauge line being traversed by Baldwin 2-8-0 No 1320, built in 1911 and still going strong!

Lenin', encircled by a standard-gauge train.

Cuba is still a major exporter of sugar products, much of it going to South America. Oil is purchased from Venezuela and in exchange Cuba sends many fully trained doctors. One of the unusual results of the communist period is that all wages, irrespective of qualifications, are the same. Now that Fidel Castro has handed the reins of power to his brother and the USA appears to be relaxing its trade embargo, necessary future investment and increased tourism is likely.

Cuba is a beautiful country with a fascinating history and exciting people, and will surely be more appreciated, but the days of the many ancient steam locomotives chugging around the cane fields is probably numbered.

Part 5: The USA

Arizona

Grand Canyon Railway

This railroad departed from the small town of Williams, Arizona, as a line branching off the single-track standard-gauge Santa Fe Pacific Railroad main line, which crosses the USA from Chicago to Los Angeles.

It must be remembered that in the 1800s the Grand Canyon, as a tourist attraction, was a far-off distant land and known only to a few explorers and the indigenous Indians such as the Hopi, Navajo and Havasupai tribes. Later that century Buckey O'Neill, Sheriff of Yavapi County, Mayor of Prescott and ardent prospector, thought that plenty of money could be made from the Anita mines some 45 miles north of Williams, and a railroad was required to transport the ore. He travelled to New York and managed to obtain the support and investment of Thomas Lombard from the investment company of Lombard, Goode & Company, and

Williams is the interchange station between the Amtrak line and the Grand Canyon Railroad. Displayed on the forecourt is three-truck Shay locomotive No 5, built in May 1923 for the Saginaw & Manistee Lumber Co.

together they entered negotiations with the Santa Fe Pacific RR.

To further whet the appetite of the Santa Fe Pacific, O'Neill tempted them with samples of gold ore that he said were from the Grand Canyon area. At the same time he began to realise the greater potential for tourism to the district and, after many months courting the Santa Fe Pacific, the railroad company capitulated and in 1897 the Grand Canyon

Railroad Company was incorporated.

Work then began to construct the 65 miles of railroad northwards from Williams through the pines and across the grasslands to the rim of the Grand Canyon. After numerous changes of management in the first year, the Atchison, Topeka & Santa Fe Railroad took control, seeing tourism as the main source of increasing income and the transport of ore as probably decreasing. The first public journey to the

Grand Canyon was made on 17 September 1901.

It was soon evident that the Grand Canyon Railroad was a winner with the tourists, and almost immediately the Santa Fe quickly started development around the rim with hotels that were at the time of the highest quality in the South West. The railroad company then built the grand depot at Williams in 1908, and located within it was one of the famous Fred Harvey hotels, the Fray Marcos Hotel, with 43 rooms and all possible facilities. Another depot was opened in 1910 at the Grand Canyon rim, built largely of logs.

The railroad thrived and was also used to transport building materials for the various hotel projects around the rim of the canyon, and until 1926 it carried necessary drinking water. Ranchers also used the railroad to transport their cattle, and lumberjacks to transport timber.

Between 1891 and 1904 there were 31 mining companies in the area, the most

Below: A passenger train with diesel No 239 stands in the ample sidings at the canyon station, once used by freight trains serving the now closed mines and timber companies.

Top: About to leave Williams is a train hauled by GM Class F-40PH diesel locomotive No 239, built in 1977 for Amtrak. It is in a striking silver and gold streamlined livery reminiscent of the 1950s.

Above: The coaches on the Grand Canyon train provide ample views of the rugged country en route to the canyon rim, together with some on-board entertainment!

productive of which was the Orphan Mine, which was situated on the southern rim of the canyon. It started life mining copper, but uranium ore was discovered and mined between 1953 and 1969; its last consignment was sent to New Mexico by rail on 23 April 1968 hauled by three locomotives, Nos 735, 1339 and 1317.

In 1968 the Grand Canyon RR closed through loss of revenue, mainly due to the interstate highway system being completed, when trucks, automobiles and coaches took over the same work. The line then fell into disrepair until 1989, when it was taken into private ownership, the track and infrastructure made good and the necessary rolling stock and locomotives obtained. The first service ran on 17 September of that same year, just 21 years after closure.

Today the Williams depot (station) is again resplendent and providing all the necessary arrival and departure facilities, although the hotel is no longer located within the building. A new Grand Canyon Railway Hotel with 297 rooms has been built immediately to the rear of the depot, and emulates the furnishings and atmosphere of bygone days. Located serenely at the left-hand side of the platform is three-truck Shay locomotive No 5, built at the Lima Works, Ohio, in 1928, which helps to set the scene. There are several carriage sidings to the right of the depot buildings. The trains are normally diesel-hauled and the journey takes 2hr 15min to the Grand Canyon depot, where there are several sidings adjacent to the passenger platform that were formerly used for the storage

Just one of hundreds of magnificent views of the colourful Grand Canyon, one of the world's most awesome spectacles.

of mining traffic and later for passenger cars. So that the whole train is facing in the right direction for its return to Williams, it is reversed out of the station and turned on a triangle before being repositioned alongside the platform.

The fleet of diesels consists of three GM Class F-40PH locomotives, Nos 237 and 239 built in 1977, and No 295 in 1979, all ex-Amtrak.

Regular steam services were withdrawn in 2008 because of environmental issues, but the two locomotives do occasionally get an outing, running on recycled vegetable oil. No 29 of Class SC-3 was built by Alco in 1906, with the regular No 4960 a 2-8-2 built by Baldwin in 1923. The latter used to work on the Midwestern Chicago, Burlington & Quincy RR into the late 1950s on freight and coal trains.

California Western Railroad

Fort Bragg is an old garrison town around 150 miles north of San Francisco on the Pacific Coast Route 1. The rugged coastal route is particularly attractive, with the wooded foothills of the Mendocino Forest stretching from the Napa Valley region around San Francisco Bay. Fort Bragg is approached across a high single-span bridge over the narrows of the sharply winding River Noyo below.

Fort Bragg is the coastal terminus of a standard-gauge former logging railway, which turns inland due east for about 40 miles to the rail junction at Willits. The lumber line was built in 1885 to bring the redwood timber, which stretches all along this part of California, to the small harbour, where sawmills were constructed. In 1904 passenger services were included, and the company's name was changed to the California Western Railroad & Navigation Company. During 1911 an interchange connection was established at Willits with the north-south North Western Pacific Railroad, running inland. In more recent years there have been several changes of ownership, with a gradual run-down of the lumber business; the Sierra Railroad acquired it in 2003, and it is now

Affectionately known as the 'Skunk Line' because of the smell of its petrol-engine railcars, this former timber railroad connects the interior woodlands with Fort Bragg and its sawmills on the Pacific coast of California. Seen here is Baldwin 2-8-2 No X45, built in October 1924.

being run as a tourist line by the Mendocino Railway. However, the line has been nicknamed the 'Skunk Train' after the petrol-engine railcars that emitted noxious fumes; one of them, No 300, was built in 1935.

The pride and joy of the 'Skunk Train' operation is its 2-8-2 locomotive No X45, built in 1924 by Baldwin for the Owen-Oregon Lumber Company. This classic loco has a

This unusual Class M300 railcar was built in 1935 by the American Car & Foundry Co and is still in operation on the line.

cow-catcher and spark-arrester chimney and of course a bell mounted behind the chimney. Its livery is ruby red with light grey panels to the cabside sheets and tender, which sports a 'Skunk' logo.

Behind the small station are several sidings, convenient parking places for a couple of rail cranes, a diesel railcar and vintage coaches awaiting restoration.

Leaving Fort Bragg the line weaves through the lovely wooded Noyo valley, along which the

Above: Willits is the terminus of the C&WRR, where sidings provide storage for several old pieces of rolling stock and this GM Class GP 9 No 4304.

Along the former logging railroad there are numerous timber trestle bridges that retain the 'old-world' character of days gone by.

Opposite page: Among the sidings at Willits were two other GM GP 9s, Nos 3844 and 3850, both having sustained costly damage to their front ends!

track crosses some 30 bridges, many of the old-style timber trestle type. No 1 bridge is 1,184 feet long and there are some 381 curves; the maximum grade is 3.5%. The summit of the line is at 1,740 feet, then it is down the gradient to Willits. Here there are still several timber sawmills at work, but the town also has the Mendocino Museum, which

has a transport interest. The North Western Pacific RR built a depot in 1915 with numerous sidings and a reversing triangle, which appears to have become a graveyard for old rolling stock and storage for several diesel locomotives.

Surprisingly, standing at the end of the triangle were two NWPRR locos, Nos 3850 and

3844, which had both been involved in some accident in which their main frames had been badly bent! The variety of wagons included bogie tank wagons and a caboose signed for 'The Redwood Route' in addition to 'cushion cars'.

A track maintenance
vehicle with trailer,
photographed at the Fort
Bragg terminus of the
California & Western
Railroad.

This old Ford van has been converted for rail use, and
usually precedes the first train of the day from Fort Bragg
to check the road is clear to Willits.

Napa Valley Railroad

The Napa Valley is now one of the premier wine-growing regions in the world, situated about 50 miles north-east of San Francisco with the town of Napa at the southern end and Calistoga at the northern end. It is approximately 30 miles north to south, and 5 miles across at its widest point.

The 42-mile single track Napa Valley Railroad (NVRR) was opened in 1868 to bring tourists to the resort town of Calistoga from Vallejo, where it connected with the San Francisco Bay ferry service. The California Pacific Railroad purchased the NVRR in 1869, and it was renamed after its owning company. It was leased to the Southern Pacific Railroad in 1885, which then purchased it in 1898. The new owner continued to run the railroad but passenger traffic ceased in 1929; freight continuing until 1987, when the railroad petitioned for abandonment. After this somewhat chequered existence, some local entrepreneurs acquired the right of way from Southern Pacific and the Napa Valley Wine Train was born!

Today's 36-mile line runs from Napa's McKinstry Street station along the fertile valley, with grapevines as far as the eye can see, to the western terminus of St Helena, beyond which the tracks have been lifted. At the Napa end the line continues south to connect with the Union Pacific and Californian Northern railroads, and

This Alco twin-unit was built in the late 1950s by the company's subsidiary, Montreal Locomotive Works, for the Canadian National Railways as Class FPA-4. Locomotive No 72 looks supreme in its period gold and red livery.

as a result occasionally hosts visiting 'Railroad Specials' and Amtrak private excursions.

This well-run railway now operates daily trains consisting of a Pullman dining car service with friendly staff in gold and ruby red uniforms that blend with the overall livery of the locomotives and coaches.

The train is usually double-headed with two diesels back to back. The railroad has four former Canadian National Railways FPA-4 Alco diesels, built by that company's Canadian subsidiary, Montreal Locomotive Works (MLW), between 1958 and 1959; they are numbered 70 to 73. The coaching stock is vintage with end balconies in true 'western' style.

From the main reception area the single track crosses a road on the level to get to the workshops. Stored here in the open are several diesel locomotives, including General California Traction switcher loco No 80, built by Alco to Class S-1. Another Alco locomotive of Class RS-11 is painted in red with three stripes of cream and blue, the

The luxurious Pullman dining coaches, built around 1915, evoke the spirit of the 1920s, with fine dining and superb local wines – a treat not to be missed.

early NVRR livery. A similar livery with slight variances adorns No 65, which sports yellow handrails and two yellow stripes.

The Napa Valley Railroad is unashamedly run as a fine restaurant, so that customers may enjoy good food served in the old-fashioned way. The passing scenery of luxuriant countryside, dotted with trees scattered among the vine groves, makes for a memorable rail journey.

Above: After a day's trip, the driver takes the power units back across the street to the motive power depot to be prepared for the next day's work.

Left: At the Californian motive depot, rescued Class RS-11 switcher diesel No 62, built in 1943 by Alco and formerly owned by the US Navy, awaits restoration.

Yosemite Mountain Sugar Pine Railroad

The Yosemite Mountain Sugar Pine Railroad (YMSPRR) is located in the dense pine forest of the Sierra Nevada, just outside the southern entrance to Yosemite National Park, at Fish Camp, California, on Route 41.

Although the YMSPRR is now a tourist attraction, it served a formidable logging area dating back to the latter part of the 19th century when the tall pines were felled by two-man teams of lumberjacks using a 10-foot-long two-handled saw and sharp axes. The great trees were then taken by horse and cart, often over difficult terrain, to the sawmill at Sugar Pine.   At the start of the 20th century a logging railway line was cut into the forest by the Madera Sugar Pine Lumber Company and used a Shay steam locomotive and specially constructed wagons to remove the massive tree trunks to the sawmill.

The Shay concept was invented and designed by Ephraim Shay, who had his own logging business in Michigan and realised that 73% of his business costs arose from moving the logs from the fell site to the sawmill using teams of horses and carts and labour, and the time it took. His new type of locomotive

This large three-truck Shay locomotive, built by Lima in 1928, is typical of the design produced to work over poorly laid and sharply curved tracks to extract timber from forest logging areas. This locomotive on the YSPRR is one of the very few Shays in regular operation.

The 'lumber' train takes passengers through the forest of redwoods and pines on the 3-foot-gauge line near the renowned Yosemite National Park. It is certainly different watching the drive shafts and bevel gears on this unusual type of locomotive.

was built by the Lima Machine Works in Ohio, and was an instant success in reducing costs for logging companies.

What is so special about a Shay? Logging areas were constantly changing, which meant quickly changing tracks or adding branches to their expanding networks, with all the imperfections that would not be allowed on a conventional railroad. The powerful Shay could handle uneven tracks, steep inclines and tight bends. Instead of a piston on either side of the locomotive, which constantly tugged the locomotive from side to side, all of its driving wheels and trucks were directly driven by shafts and bevel gears from three cylinders and pistons located on the side of the locomotive. Its adhesion to the rails was akin to that of a 4x4 vehicle of today. It was also built to the 3-foot (914mm) narrow gauge for tight bends. The other major benefit was that all the important moving parts were located on the outside of the locomotive, allowing maintenance and repairs to be carried out on-site.

In 1961 a family concern reconstructed a small part of the Madera lumber railroad on the former trackbed. Once the winding track had been laid, a three-truck Shay locomotive, No 10, built in 1928, was acquired; it was one of the last to be built at Lima, Ohio, and is considered to be the largest Shay type. In 1986 another Shay was bought, No 15, which, like No 10, had worked for the West Side Lumber Company and Cherry Valley Railroad in Tuolumne. No 15, also a three-truck loco, was completed on 20 May 1913. Both Shays are oil-burners with a capacity of 830 imperial gallons (3,800 litres) of oil, and 1,700 imperials gallons (7,600 litres) of water.   To supplement the two Shays, the tourist line has two Ford Model A automobiles converted to carry 12 passengers. Also running as required is No 402, a centre-cab two-truck diesel, and No 5, a two-axle switcher diesel built in 1935. Among the rolling stock is a rare narrow-gauge snowplough. Passengers are taken on trips through the pine forest in open bogie wagons – with seats!

Cumbres & Toltec Scenic Railroad

The Denver & Rio Grande Railroad (D&RG) was incorporated in the Territories of Colorado and New Mexico in October 1870 to build its railroads using the 3-foot gauge instead of the 4ft 8½in standard gauge. This narrow gauge was chosen because construction was cheaper and equipment less expensive, and it allowed much tighter curves to be used in the more mountainous areas. Gradually the narrow-gauge network spread across the territories, providing freight transport for timber, livestock, fruit and mining products, as well as passenger services. The D&RG narrow-gauge network peaked at 1,861 miles of track, with some major routes being converted to standard gauge during the 1880s.

By the 1950s an increasing amount of freight was being transported by road and the Denver & Rio Grande Western Railroad (D&RGW), as it was later called, went into decline; by the early 1960s the narrow-gauge network had been closed down.

The Cumbres & Toltec Scenic Railroad (C&TSRR) is now listed as a preserved historic site, and trains run between the eastern terminus at Antonito, Colorado, west to the terminus at Chama, New Mexico, a journey of

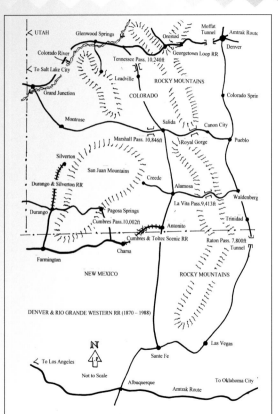

The Cumbres & Toltec Scenic, Durango & Silverton and Georgetown Loop railroads and their surrounding lines (not to scale).

64 miles. From Antonito the train climbs 2,134 feet to the summit at Cumbres (10,002 feet), then descends to Chama.

Apart from the narrow-gauge lines, the D&RGW had a substantial standard-gauge network, and probably the last remaining section of dual-track, standard- and 3-foot gauges remains in use at Antonito. The reason for this is that on the flat high plains surrounding Antonito there is a perlite factory, which distributes its product by standard gauge all over the USA. Perlite is a volcanic rock similar to granite, and is quarried near No Agua, New Mexico. The rock is heated, crushed and graded as a lightweight aggregate used in cement and in oil drilling, and as a filtering agent in drugs and chemicals.

The original Antonito depot was built in 1880 near the junction of the standard-gauge Santa Fe line to New Mexico and the narrow-gauge line to Durango, Colorado. All the current timber buildings were constructed in 1970, including the two-road engine shed. In that year the C&TSRR acquired the line to Chama from the D&RGW.

The sidings at Antonito contain an assortment of cattle trucks and box cars in addition to the vintage red-painted coaches, some with verandas.

Above: Baldwin 2-8-2 No 487, a Class K-36 2-8-2 built in 1925, is about to leave Antonito, where the narrow-gauge line meets the standard gauge of the Denver & Rio Grande Railroad, with joint gauge track in the foreground.

Leaving the upland plains of semi-arid desert covered in sage brush, the line continues to ascend through aspen groves and pine trees. Passing through the San Juan Mountains, the line hugs cliff edges towards the canyon, keeping a steady 20mph. In the past some silver-mining was carried out in this hill country, but its demise came about when the Government agreement to purchase all silver production was rescinded, causing a slump and loss of revenue to the railway.

About halfway along the line, the trains that have set out in each direction stop at Osier for an hour. This permits passengers to have lunch and a comfort stop. Spectacular views of the mountains are obtained and, when the trains pass in the loop, one can watch as the departing train winds its way around the hillside across the valley. At Osier, water is taken on, as this was a former section house with a snow house covering a 60-foot loco turntable, which permitted shorter runs up from Chama to take in the lovely views.

This is the view across the Osier Gorge, where there is a passing loop for trains to pass. The train in the distance is heading for Antonito, and is seen from a train heading towards Chama.

The train then reaches the Cumbres summit at 10,002 feet, then starts its sharp descent towards Chama, passing over the state line into New Mexico. Chama was a railway town of some importance and today is one of the few stations that still has an elevated coal plant, built in 1924, the last one in use. Nearby there was formerly a six-road roundhouse with a 50-foot turntable, but these were demolished in 1940. The present engine shed has only two stalls. The sidings hold a selection of rolling stock consisting of box wagons and an interesting snowplough, all painted in bauxite brown.

Above: Baldwin No 487 is working hard on its ascent towards Osier as it takes the train of vintage clerestory coaches around the tight curves in the rocky hills of New Mexico.

Left: An example of a North American bi-directional upper-quadrant semaphore signal at Cumbres.

During D&RGW times the line continued from Chama with a northerly branch to Pagosa Springs, then the narrow-gauge main line continued west towards Durango and Silverton.

Locomotive power on the C&TSRR consists of five Class K-36 2-8-2 'Mikado' steam locomotives, Nos 483, 484, 487 and 489, built by the Baldwin Locomotive Works in 1925. Like their sisters on the Durango system, they were used on freight trains throughout the D&RGW narrow-gauge system.

Far right: The train makes its way towards the summit of this scenic railroad at Cumbres, at 10,002 feet, having climbed 2,134 feet from Antonito.

Above right: Chama station still retains a 'film set' appearance with its ancient coal plant and wooden water tank still used by the steam locomotives.

Right: A track maintenance vehicle with trailers on the Cumbres & Toltec. Can't leave anything behind – I might need it!

Durango & Silverton Railroad

The Durango & Silverton Railroad (D&SRR), located in the San Juan Mountains of Colorado, was a 45-mile branch of the Denver & Rio Grande Railroad 3-foot narrow gauge network (see previous section) that weaved its way around Colorado (and New Mexico). The branch was opened in 1882, having taken only 11 months to construct, supplied the mining town of Silverton with food, construction materials and mining supplies, and remained flourishing for the next 30 years or so. The population of Silverton had more than doubled to 2,000-plus by 1885.

Durango was on the main narrow-gauge line that linked, in an easterly direction, with Chama, then over the Cumbres summit to Antonito, before running on to Alamosa, where a change to a standard-gauge train was required for the onward journey to Denver.

However, all good things come to an end and by the 20th century much of the narrow-gauge had been abandoned. Profitability had been hard hit and track maintenance reduced, so much so that the Denver & Rio Grande Western Railroad (D&RGW) had the nickname of 'Dangerous and Rapidly Growing Worse'. Faster and more direct standard-gauge routes had been constructed, leaving the narrow-gauge network isolated and unpopular.

Today, the Durango & Silverton Narrow Gauge Railroad (D&SNGR) is in private

Alco Class K-36 2-8-2 No 481, built in 1925, is one of four that work the D&SRR stabled in the original roundhouse at Durango, now partly a museum.

ownership and the entire line is a National Historic Landmark.

Durango has an attractive depot (station), a rail museum and a wonderful roundhouse with a working turntable. There are plenty of wagons and a couple of derelict-looking steam locomotives in sidings at the rear of the yard. Two diesel locomotives are used to assemble

the coaches for the trains while the steam locomotives are coaled and watered. Some of the coaches here are believed to be the oldest in the USA, dating from the 1880s.

The journey from Durango takes 3½ hours, following the fast-flowing Animas River. The canyon scenery is nothing but spectacular, and sometimes the rails run close to the roaring river, hanging on to cliff edges and ever climbing higher into the mountains. At Hermosa a water stop is made and if the train is to be double-headed to Silverton, the second engine backs down onto the front locomotive. When crossing the bridge over the Animas River the locos usually 'blow-down' to clear water from the cylinders before hitting the continuously changing curves and steep gradients where 2.5% and 3.0% are not uncommon.

Arriving at Silverton, the train runs along the side of the main road and terminates just before the crossroads in the middle of the town! The remains of several silver mines on the steep hills with their spoil tips can be seen, giving the town its name. There is a stopover here of 2¼ hours, and the broad streets, wooden sidewalks and honky-tonk bars provide a very pleasant lunch break in this typical 'western' saloon town, where a beer goes down well with the sound of the old music hall piano.

Before returning to Durango the train reverses to a triangle on the fringes of Silverton, allowing it to be repositioned, locomotive in front, facing the downhill run to Durango. Having reversed back up the main road, it stops, ready for its passengers to board for the return journey.

The steam locomotives used on the D&SRR are of the 2-8-2 configuration and of two classes. Class K-28 is rated at 27,500lb force and consists of Nos 473, 476 and 478. The K-36 series are Nos 480, 481, 482 and 486, rated at 36,000lb force. The K-28s were built by the Schenectady Locomotive Works (Alco) in 1923 and the

Having left the town of Durango behind, the 3-foot-gauge line runs for much of its 45-mile ascent to Silverton following the Animas River, which it crosses several times, often in deep gorges.

K-36s by Baldwin in 1925. There are three centre-cab diesels with a fourth undergoing restoration. 'Hotshot', No 1, was built in 1957 for the Arkansas Limestone RR, and 'Big Al', No 7, in 1975 for the Algoma Steel Co of Michigan.

Nos 9 and 11, built by General Electric, were purchased in 2006.

The grade up from the valley towards Silverton takes the railway via precarious rocky ledges near Rockwood. Here the train is seen approaching the tightest curve (28 degrees), some 240 feet (73m) above the Animas River.

Top left: Double-headed by Alco 2-8-2s Nos 478 and 473, the train comes to a halt in the centre of Silverton, just 50 yards from the main street. No station, platform or buffer stops here – the track just ends in the gravel.

Above: Having climbed 2,796 feet to get to the old mining town of Silverton, passengers have time to explore the broad main street, seen in several films, with its old cars and honky-tonk bars.

Left: Cabooses, or bogie brake vans, were once a familiar sight in the States. The one in the foreground at Silverton's freight museum is from the local Rio Grande RR and the other from the Sante Fe.

Georgetown Loop Railroad

Situated just off Interstate 70 in Colorado, about 45 miles (72km) west of Denver, are two old mining towns, Georgetown and Silver Plume, tucked within the wild and rugged Rocky Mountains. These two small towns lie 2 miles apart in Clear Creek Valley and tourists come to ride the train that connects them. It is a unique experience trundling over the 3-foot narrow-gauge track, rounding the curves and taking in the view down the creek from the Devil's Gate High Bridge. The total journey is just over 3 miles (5km), the 'corkscrew' route rising more than 600 feet (183m) from Devils Gate station at Georgetown to Silver Plume. Although this heritage line now operates in isolation, the short journey is well worth a visit.

In the summer of 1859, following the great gold rush, a certain George Griffiths discovered gold in Clear Creek and a small and growing settlement began, known as 'Georges Town'. By 1864 the gold-mining era had come to an end and silver was then discovered in the area. Georgetown was now overflowing with miners and tourists, but there was no railroad connecting it to Denver to transport passengers or the millions of dollars-worth of ore from the mines.

Eventually, the Colorado Central Railroad built the line and it was opened completely in 1884 when it reached Silver Plume. By this time silver-mining was on the wane and Georgetown

An old photo, circa 1890, of a train crossing the precarious-looking Devil's Gate High Bridge.

was benefiting more from tourism, with regular railroad excursions.

With the advent of the motor car the railroad business declined rapidly and the last trains ran from Denver in 1938. The Georgetown to Silver Plume loop was abandoned and dismantled, including the Devil's Gate High Bridge. By 1940 the local silver mines had also closed.

In 1973 the Colorado Historical Society

began to restore the railroad and build a new bridge as part of its 978-acre Georgetown Loop Historic Mining and Railroad Park.

Today the Georgetown Loop Railroad (GLRR) relies on tourism, but the trip over the new Devil's Gate High Bridge should not be missed. Silver Plume station is the main terminus, with sidings for rolling stock, a run-round loop and workshops.

The steam locomotive used is a Shay type (3199) built in 1923 by the Lima Locomotive Works in Ohio. This narrow-gauge loco has a rather odd one-sided look, as the boiler is positioned to the right of the frames, with the three cylinders and pistons arranged vertically side-by-side down the left-hand side. This arrangement allows for a direct and flexible drive to all the wheels through a combination of gears. Overall, the engine is a balanced and powerful 80-ton unit producing 36,150lb tractive effort. This type of locomotive was ideal for the logging industry, as it was able to negotiate forests on hurriedly laid track and haul the giant logs back to the mill. Although these locomotives were powerful they had no great turn of speed. This example spent its working life with the West Coast Lumber Co working out of Tuolumne, California, and was designated No 9.

There are two diesel locomotives. Narrow-gauge diesel-electric locomotive No 1203 was built by H. K. Porter & Co of Pittsburgh as No 8096 in 1947. It weighs 87 tons, and has six axles with six Westinghouse electric motors powered from a six-cylinder Alco diesel engine producing

The mainstay of the locomotive fleet on the line is diesel-electric No 1203 built by H. K. Porter of Pittsburgh in 1947, seen here in the yard at Silver Plume. It is well turned out in black with orange chevrons on the front end.

660hp. Its working life was with US Gypsum in Plaster City until 1979, and it was then sold to the Huckleberry Railroad in Flint, Michigan. It was sold to the GLRR in May 2008. The other narrow-gauge diesel electric locomotive is No 21, built in the 1940s by General Electric; it weighs

44 tons and is used on the GLRR for back-up operations and general duties in the yard. Until the 1980s it pulled wagonloads of steel ingots at the Rocky Mountain Steel Mills of Pueblo. It then sat idle until 2004, when it was donated to the Colorado Historical Society.

Apart from the locomotives there are five open gondolas, two covered gondolas and three box cars from the Denver and Rio Grande Western Railroad. There are also a number of wagons, including a D&RGW caboose.

The round trip is about 1hr 15min and quite spectacular. There is also the old Lebanon Silver Mine in the park, where visitors can walk 500 feet into the mine's tunnel, bored in the 1870s – a must-do!

Above: The train carefully negotiates the curve of the new Devil's Gate High Bridge. It's a long way down!

Left: Having crossed the bridge and travelled round the loop, the train passes underneath it as it continues its descent towards Devil's Gate station.

Index of locations

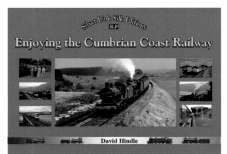